The Lie of the Land

The Lie of the Land

Irish Identities

FINTAN O'TOOLE

VERSO

London · New York

First published by Verso 1997
© Fintan O'Toole 1997
Paperback edition published by Verso 1999
All rights reserved

Verso
UK: 6 Meard Street, London W1V 3HR
USA: 180 Varick Street, New York NY 10014–4606

Verso is the imprint of New Left Books

ISBN 1–85984–821–4
ISBN 1–85984–132–5 (pbk)

British Library Cataloguing in Publication Data
A catalogue record for this book is available from the British Library

Library of Congress Cataloging-in-Publication Data
A catalog record for this book is available from the Library of Congress

Typeset by SetSystems Ltd, Saffron Walden, Essex
Printed by Biddles Ltd, Guildford and King's Lynn

Contents

Acknowledgements

These pieces, which together try to describe what it feels like to be Irish in the 1990s, are a mixture of journalism and essays. Almost all of them start from news items, radio interviews, political speeches – the flotsam and jetsam of the public world. If they make use of history, or of art, it is only as surfboards on which to try to stay upright while the waves of events rush forward. I make no claim to detachment from the immediacy of things as they happen, not only because I am first and foremost a journalist, but also because the culture being described here is one which is still in the process of emergence.

Many of these pieces, indeed, were written for *The Irish Times* as responses to immediate political circumstances – elections, scandals, referenda. I have left them as they were published first, since whatever value they have is inextricable from the times and the events to which they respond. I am very grateful to *The Irish Times*, to its editor Conor Brady and to Liam McAuley, Dick Grogan, Joe Breen, Sean Flynn, Patsey Murphy, Caroline Walsh, Paddy Woodworth and Peter Murtagh, both for publishing them in the first place and for giving me permission to re-publish them here.

The Lie of the Land was developed in part for the Oriel Gallery in Cardiff, in part for the New Tate Gallery in Liverpool, and in yet another part for the Glenstal Ecumenical Conference in 1993. An earlier version of *Going Native* was written for the SOFEIR conference in Lyon in 1993. *Meanwhile Back at the Ranch* was written as a lecture for the Canadian Association for Irish Studies in 1990. Many of these ideas, in turn, were developed for the BBC Radio 4 series *Notes from Laputa*, produced by Mary Price, which I wrote in 1993.

Acknowledgements

All of the essays in this book have been published in Ireland by Raven Arts Press and New Island Books in three separate volumes – *A Mass for Jesse James*; *Black Hole, Green Card*; and *The Ex-Isle of Erin*. I am immensely grateful to Dermot Bolger, Edwin Higel, Anthony Glavin and Frances O'Rourke for the work they did on those books, and to Jane Hindle for her work on this selection.

As ever, I owe a lifetime's gratitude to Clare Connell for her patience, forebearance and companionship.

for Kieran, Mary, Valerie and Patrick

Introduction

My parents' wedding photographs always remind me of a frontier town in an old Western. To prise open the mock mother-of-pearl covers of the wedding album is to enter a world of strange contrasts. There they are, elegant and radiant, wrapped in the proud formality of the 1950s, the elaborate dress and veil, the clean lines of my father's bespoke suit. They are emblems of a great continuity, of a seriousness and respectability forged over generations of struggle against squalor and dirt, against poverty and fecklessness. Their adamant dignity sparkles like a diamond hard-won from the dust and muck.

What gives the pictures their air of *High Noon*, though, of a respectable wedding threatened by the dangers of a frontier town, is the setting. The church, which should be dark with gothic curves or bright with baroque tracery, is merely dull with the blank stare of unadorned concrete. It is not really a church at all, but a temporary building slapped up to serve a hastily conceived new suburb while the real one is still being built. It has no grace and no resonance. It may have been consecrated by the wave of a bishop's hand, but it is unconsecrated by those holier things, by the skill of craftsmen or by the hopes and dreams of generations. Yet, for me, because of those photographs, it has to serve as one of those images of tradition and remembrance that we all carry around in our heads.

That ramshackle place, raw and temporary and forever unfinished, has to serve as the locus of an ordered secure past. Strangely, though it still looks temporary after forty years, it is still there, still an ugly shell of windowless breeze-block with a reinforced steel door at one side. And while the huge, windy church that replaced it now looks dated, ineffably of its time, the very blankness and ugliness of the temporary structure make it curiously timeless. Built without design or intention, it is not marked by the designs or intentions of any one decade. It could be the newest public building on the estate instead of the oldest. While families and lives come and go around it, it abides, a monument to the permanently temporary nature of the new Ireland whose frontier it once occupied.

With time, indeed, the building took on its own eerie importance. There was something strange about having this deconsecrated church down the road from the real one. It had the mysterious, ghostly presence of a wrecked ship at the mouth of a busy harbour, or a deserted village chanced upon in the quiet hills. And, indeed, it became a kind of alternative church, a site for a different sort of communion entered into by the disaffected young, the holy bread of sex and the heady wine of rock and roll. When I was about ten, the modern world, in all its shocking glory, arrived at this now-secularised church.

What happened was ordinary enough in its beginnings but deeply shocking in its repercussions. It began as a set of actions from the 1950s and ended as one from the 1980s. On a Wednesday evening in 1968, at the youth club hop in that still-temporary building where my parents were married, a priest arrived to find the lights down low and the couples clinched in too-sinful embrace. The dance was broken up, the dancers sent home. It was a small and clichéd drama, a tired reprise of a scene played out in parish halls and at crossroads all over the old Catholic Ireland. It was the shocking response to it that marked, for us, the death of that Ireland.

Instead of burning with shame as the scandal was whispered around the parish, the dancers muttered together and let their anger fester. At ten o'clock Mass the next Sunday, they acted. They arrived early and en masse, and sat in the front two rows, facing the pulpit. As the parish priest rose for his sermon, they stood up and walked out, down the centre aisle, past gaping mothers and spluttering fathers, stilling the fingers that told the beads and silencing the lips that mouthed the pious murmurs. They would come back a few weeks later, defeated and cowed, never realising that they had dragged a whole world behind them in their footsteps when they walked out that door. They lost the battle but won a war they hardly knew they were fighting.

It is said that Haile Selassie's reign as emperor of Ethiopia ended, not when he was eventually overthrown by the army, but when, a few years earlier, a disaffected young official whom he was removing from his post turned and walked out of the palace, not backwards and bowing, as custom demanded, but with his back to the emperor and his head held high. From that moment the empire was doomed. In the same way, and with the same inevitability, an empire of certainties was doomed in our parish that day. An authority had been lost and could never be regained.

In 1992, fifteen years after I had moved out of the parish, my eye was drawn to a newspaper headline. 'Priest shocked over rave drugs party held in parish bingo hall', it said. 'A Dublin priest', went the first paragraph, 'who hired out his parish hall for a "fiftieth wedding anniversary" at the weekend was shocked to discover it was used for a rave acid house party instead, which was raided by gardai.' The hall, of course, was that same temporary building in which my parents were married and from which the beginning of the disappearance of an old Ireland took, for us, its local habitation and its name.

The incident was a wilder, more dramatic, but somehow less significant replay of those events of twenty-five years ago. The noise had woken people in the surrounding houses in the small hours of Sunday morning. The police had been called. At 2 a.m., the ravers locked the doors with two hundred people inside and the Ecstasy-driven dancing continued for three hours.

Finally, after dawn, the police and the parish priest stormed the hall. The priest took to the stage under the flashing lights and screamed at the dancers to stop. No one minded his distress very much. The police dismantled the sound equipment and the lighting rig and took it all away. The dancers yawned and went out into the early light that was washing the playing fields a new bright green. It was Sunday morning and time for bed.

The temporary hall had finally triumphed over the permanent church. The contingent, makeshift society was now more real than the illusions of permanence and tradition. The parish priest, not the young dancers in the hall, was now the lonely protester, the bewildered voice crying out in the flashing light.

The Republic of Ireland in which my parents got married was still a known country. In the time between my parents' wedding and the all-night rave, that capacity to know itself had gradually been lost to Ireland. The fixed points on the compass of life – Church, nation, family – had been unsettled. In three decades Ireland became a place where much more was known about individual lives, but where larger realities became literally unknown. In the globalised Irish economy of the 1990s – three quarters of Irish manufactured exports are from foreign-owned transnational corporations – the Ireland invented by nineteenth-century nationalists could not hold together.

Likewise, the relative stability of the population figures – currently about 3.6 million – conceals a continuing instability of inflows and outflows. Emigration has been the single biggest fact in the 75-year history of the Irish State. Only half of those born in Ireland in the early 1930s, for instance, were still living there thirty years later. The rate of emigration dropped rapidly in the 1960s, but picked up again in the late 1970s and early 1980s, so that the 1996 census showed that nearly 20 per cent of those born in 1970 were by then living in some other country. Some of these people went and stayed gone. Some came back, left again, returned again. Some of those who went were themselves the children of emigrants who returned in the 1960s. In 1996, too, three quarters of a million Irish residents paid visits to relatives living abroad: home, for the Irish, is not necessarily where the heart is.

Introduction

'A nation', says Leopold Bloom in James Joyce's *Ulysses*, 'is the same people living in the same place.' And then, under pressure, he adds 'Or also living in different places.' Ireland invented itself under the auspices of the first of those attempted definitions. The conjunction of 'same people' and 'same place', conveniently reinforced by the partition of the island which created separate Catholic and Protestant domains, made a thing called 'Ireland'. Now, as we face the disappearance of that Ireland under the pressures of economics, of geography, of the collapse of the religious monolith which was inseparable from our self-definition, we are left with no option but to add Bloom's contradictory corrective about different places. And even that may not be enough. We live in different places, but are we the 'same people'? Only if we can understand sameness in a way that incorporates difference, that brooks contradictions, and that is comfortable with the idea that the only fixed Irish identity and the only useful Irish tradition is the Irish tradition of not having a fixed identity.

One of the things that helped to give the illusion of a fixity to an identity that was actually in perpetual motion was the availability of an overwhelming Other – England – by contrast with which Ireland could be defined. But in 1996, arguably for the first time in recorded Irish history, it became impossible to understand the Republic of Ireland by reference to Britain. It was no longer possible to blame British colonialism, the nightmare of a benighted past, for the country's problems. It was no longer possible to envisage Ireland as merely the other side of England. Seventy-five years after the signing, on 6 December 1921, of the Anglo-Irish Treaty establishing the Irish Free State, Ireland lost one of the key ingredients of its political and cultural make-up. After centuries of imagining itself in the shadow of a bigger, more powerful, and above all richer neighbour, it was faced with the necessity, not just to think again, but to find a whole new way of thinking. In terms of mental geography, Ireland ceased to be an island off Britain.

In 1996, the Republic of Ireland produced more wealth per head of population than the United Kingdom. As recently as the early 1970s, after the last great boom time for the Irish economy, gross domestic product (GDP) per head of population in the Republic was half that of the UK. But if the EU average for GDP per head was 100, for 1996 the figures were 100.7 for Ireland and 98.9 for the UK. And this gap is expected to widen so that in 1998 it will be 106.3 for Ireland and 99.6 for the UK.

Samuel Beckett's jokey reply to the question '*Vous êtes Anglais, Monsieur Beckett?*' ('You are English, Mr Beckett?') – '*Au contraire*' – no longer works. What *Newsweek* magazine described in December 1996 as the 'Emerald Tiger' economy was not so much on the prowl as on the razzle-dazzle. For those who could afford the entrance fee, Ireland had entered the world's fair of global consumerism. It belonged, with Britain and the rest of western Europe, in the developed world.

Normally, those who preside over such good times could expect to bask in the glow of national gratitude. Instead, the opposite has been the case. As wealth grew, so did an extraordinary popular scepticism about leaders of all sorts, to such an extent that the whole idea of authority – political, moral, religious – became utterly problematic. The authority of the State itself had been eroded, at least partly because the public no longer seemed to associate good times with national politics at all. Ministers may have gotten to spend the billions of pounds flowing in from the EU's regional and social funds, but the public knew that it had people outside the State – mostly German taxpayers – to thank for them. Ministers may have gotten to announce huge industrial investments like IBM's 3,000-job project for Dublin or Intel's $1.5 billion investment in Leixlip, but the public knew that the real decisions had been taken on the far side of the Atlantic.

This is the paradox of the Republic of Ireland in the aftermath of the British Empire – its national independence is underwritten by transnational corporations and by a supra-national European

Union. Its sovereignty is a power that can be exercised mostly by giving it up. Its separation three quarters of a century ago from one political and economic union, the United Kingdom, is justified by its membership of a bigger political and economic union, the EU. Its cultural distinctiveness lies not in any fixed inherited tradition but in the particular way that it reacts to an overload of global stimuli, taking possession of Anglo-American norms, putting its own stamp on them and exporting them back to England, America and the rest of the world.

The purpose of these essays is to suggest three things about globalisation. One is that that process is having a profound effect on Irish culture. A second is that justified complaints about 'American cultural imperialism' can sometimes miss the point that American mass culture may well contain buried elements of other cultures. This is particularly so in the case of Ireland, and it is one of the reasons why multinational pop culture can be used creatively, rather than merely consumed, by Irish people. The third is that globalisation is not a one-way process. It affects different cultures in different ways, and each culture also makes its own contribution to the shape of global forces. Because it has been in a real sense a global society long before the term 'globalisation' was ever heard, this is especially true of Ireland. It has buried memories, forgotten histories, that offer it some useful precedents for engaging with, rather than being swamped by, the new realities. By remembering and re-imagining them, it can, perhaps, learn how to surf the global waves without drowning in a flood tide of blandness and amnesia.

The essays in this book are an attempt to explore some of the ways in which the disappearance of a fixed Irish identity and the emergence of a set of provisional, contingent identities has manifested itself in Irish life in the 1990s. They deal with politics, history, landscape, religion and culture. But they do not pretend to deal with any of these areas comprehensively. Their aim is to be suggestive and exploratory rather than comprehensive or dogmatic. They were written, as Leopold Bloom's definition of nation is given, under pressure of events; and in full awareness that at any moment it will be necessary to add 'Or also . . .'

The Lie of the Land

Some Thoughts on the Map of Ireland

1.

In January 1994 the Irish Post Office moved its sorting oper-
ations on to a new computerised system. Problems began when
the computer started reading the first place name on each
address as the crucial one, so that letters for Dublin Road,
Galway went to Dublin and letters for Cork Street, Dublin went
to Cork. On RTE radio, the company's chief executive admitted
that a letter addressed to a house called Arizona somewhere in
the Midlands went to Arizona. Who is to say that the computer
was not right, that the confusion was not, in its own way, a
kind of truth?

In May 1993 the Committee of Public Accounts of Dail
Eireann discovered that Ireland had disappeared. Or rather, that
85,000 Irelands had disappeared. James V. Rogers, accounting
officer of the Ordnance Survey, told the committee that 85,000
maps of Ireland were mysteriously unaccounted for. A stock-
taking in March 1992 had shown up this discrepancy between
the number of maps sold and the number actually in stock. The
committee spent an hour pondering the question of what might
have happened to so many representations of the country.

Sean Doherty, the former Fianna Fáil Minister for Justice
whose revelations about phone tapping had led to the downfall
of Charles Haughey as Taoiseach in early 1992, took a particular interest in the question. Was it possible, he asked, that the
maps might never have existed?

'Yes,' said Mr Rogers, 'that is possible.'

'There is no loss of something that never existed,' said Sean Doherty.

But if they had existed, wondered Senator Martin Cullen, how much space would they have taken up? After all, you could hardly hide that many Irelands in a corner somewhere. Maybe they had been spirited away?

Supposing the maps did occupy space, Sean Doherty insisted, how much space would it be?

'Do you mean linear footage?' asked Mr Rogers.

And so the metaphysicians pondered, looking for their lost country, until, in the end, Sean Doherty brought the discussion to a close with the warning that 'We may have to search where we never searched before.'

This comic mystery story, staged at the heart of political power in Ireland, was more than usually symbolic. These disappeared Irelands, these lost maps of the island, these questions of how much space something that does not exist might take up, expressed in their own way a real sense of a place that has slipped away. A map, after all, is a convenient fiction, a more or less confident representation of the shape a place might take if only you could see it. While the place itself persists, the map, the visual and ideological convention that allows us to call that place 'Ireland' has been slipping away. Its co-ordinates, its longitudes and latitudes, refuse to hold their shape.

2.

In this Chart, I have laide down no land nor figur'd out any shore but what I saw myself, and thus far the Chart may be depended on.
– The Journals of Captain James Cook On His Voyages Of Discovery, 1768–1771

On the original map of the eastern shores of Australia charted on Captain Cook's Endeavour voyage, a large undulating band of letters follows the course of the carefully plotted coast. The letters form the words NEW SOUTH WALES, DISC. 1770. They are written more or less vertically, from the bottom up, but they twist in a graceful double arc. They curve inwards from Bateman Bay to Point Danger, as the coast does, and then, like the coast, curve outward again towards Cape Cleveland, before tapering outwards again to Trinity Bay. When these words were written on the map, borrowing the name of a submerged country thousands of miles away, the place they gave that name to was largely unknown to those who wrote them. And indeed, with their shape that describes a voyage, they seem to refer not to a fixed place at all, but to a journey that has just been made. Looking at them, you realise that the map, as Paul Carter has pointed out, 'was from the beginning, designed to record particular information. As the spaces on its grid were written over, there was revealed a palimpsest of the explorer's experience, a criss-cross of routes gradually thickening and congealing into fixed seas and lands. In this context, the rubric "New South Wales, Disc. 1770" named not so much a country but, by the direction of its writing, the course of a journey.'

This serpentine rubric on a map of exploration, naming the course of a journey but reminiscent of a remembered place called Wales, seems appropriate to Ireland in the 1990s. These literally twisted words, projecting the name of a historic place on to a blank and uncharted space, belong to what Carter calls 'Cook's geo-graphy, his writing of lands', a similar geography to that in which the Irish are now engaged. If they lay out a country, it is, as Cook boasted, 'no land but what I saw myself', a country whose map is no more nor less than the chart of personal experience and personal journeys. In a country like Ireland, whose modern history is shaped by the personal journeys of the emigrant, any accurate map of the land must be a map, not of an island, but of a shoreline seen from the water, a set of contours shaped, not by geography, but by voyages. The shape of the island is the shape of all the journeys around it that a history of emigration has set in motion.

As it happens, modern geometry has given a new sanction to this kind of subjective map-making. In his *Fractal Geometry of Nature*, the mathematician Benoit Mandlebrot asks the apparently simple question 'How long is the coast of Britain?' The coast is obviously not smooth and regular. It goes in and out in bays and estuaries and promontories and capes. If you measure it at one hundred miles to an inch, all of these irregularities appear. But if you measure it at twenty miles to an inch, new bays open up on the coastlines of promontories and new promontories jut out from the sides of bays. When you measure these as well, the coastline gets longer. At a mile to an inch it is even longer ... and so on, until you crawl around on your hands and knees measuring the bumps on the side of each rock that makes up the coast. The more accurately you measure it, the more uncertain it becomes. What matters, in the end, is your point of view. Mandlebrot compares the length of the border between Spain and Portugal in a Portuguese and a Spanish atlas. In the former it is 20 per cent longer than in the latter, not because the territory is disputed, but because Spanish surveyors used a larger scale, and thus measured fewer squiggles.

So it is with the map of Ireland. The closer you look, the more accurately you take into account the actual experiences of the people born on the island, the more unstable the coastline becomes. Subjectively, using the small scale to measure the inlets and outflows of human life, the coastline expands to breaking point, scattering the inhabitants of the island half way around the globe.

Emigration means, quite simply, that the people and the land are no longer co-terminous. In this sense, the map of Ireland is a lie. The lie of the land is that there is a place called 'Ireland' inhabited by the Irish people, a place with a history, a culture, a society. Yet the central fact of that history is that, over 150 years, much of it has happened elsewhere, in Chicago and Coventry, in Boston and Birmingham, in Hell's Kitchen and Camden Town. The central fact of that culture is that it knows no borders. The central fact of that society is that it is porous and diffuse, that its apparent stability is maintained only at the cost of the continual export of its instabilities.

It was an Irishman, Oscar Wilde, who wrote that 'a map of the world that does not include Utopia is not worth even glancing at, for it leaves out the one country at which humanity is always landing. And, when humanity lands there, it looks out, and seeing a better country, sets sail.' In a more downbeat mood, one can say that a map of Ireland that does not include its elsewheres is not worth even glancing at, for it leaves out the places where Ireland is always landing and returning from.

The map of the world that illustrates Myles na Gopaleen's 1941 Irish-language novel *An Béal Bocht* (*The Poor Mouth*) is thus as accurate as it is funny. Drawn by the artist Sean O'Sullivan, it represents 'the great world as it appears to the people of Corca Dorcha', na Gopaleen's satiric peasant Ireland. In the middle is Ireland, an island with but a few features marked: Corca Dorcha, Sligo Jail, Dublin and Cork (containing 'gentlefolk'), and a small piece towards the North marked 'Orangemen'. To the west is a similar sized island called Thar Lear (Overseas), which has long-horn cattle, money order offices for emigrants' remittances, and three cities in the east: New York, Boston and Springfield, Mass. To the east is a third island called De Odar Saighd, which has money order offices, George Bernard Shaw and a long bit at the top containing a money order office and a section marked 'Gaelic spoken here', reached by routes marked 'pratie hokers' routes'. The compass on the map has four directions: West, West, West and West.

The book's other illustration, set in the text, is The Sea Cat, the terrible monster that assails the hero in one of his darkest hours. Unable to describe it in words, he draws it on a piece of paper. It is an outline map of Ireland on its side, the four great peninsulas of the west coast underneath as legs, Ulster a head, Wexford the tail. He is told that it is a horrible creature that comes ashore only to do evil, and that no one has seen it before and lived. The map of Ireland has become a comically monstrous creature, appearing now and then from the waves of the Atlantic, bringing nothing but misfortune in its wake.

The real map of such a place is etched into faces, since only the personal histories of emigrants accurately describe it. Eugene O'Neill, in his final reckoning with his emigrant past, *Long Day's Journey Into Night*, has his father's alter ego James Tyrone snap at his son, who has been bad-mouthing Ireland, 'Keep your dirty tongue off Ireland! You're a fine one to sneer, with the map of it on your face!' That map imprinted on a face, whose contours shift, with smiles and frowns, is the most truthful map of Ireland there is.

Another such image is that near the end of Sam Shepard's play *A Lie of the Mind*. Two women, mother and daughter, are adrift in the modern American wilderness. They are preparing to set out and leave their lives behind, one sorting through old letters and photographs to decide what is junk, the other leafing through travel brochures. Suddenly the mother holds up a 'big colourful map of Ireland', points to it and exclaims 'I found it. Here it is. Right here. Sligo County. Connaught.' She remembers a name – 'Skellig. Mary Skellig, and there was a Shem or Sham or somethin' like that' – but she has never been to the place. Her only knowledge of it is that 'I used to remember my grandma talk about it.' The Skelligs are 'Relatives. Ancestors. I don't know.' Maybe, her daughter suggests, they are all dead. 'People don't just all die. They don't just all up and die at once unless it's a catastrophe or somethin'. Someone's always left behind to carry on.' And out of this vague sense that someone must be left behind, on the basis of this map of an unknown country, they stake their future on a trip to Ireland.

Between these two images of the map of Ireland – an indelible stain of the past on the face of the present, and a risky act of faith in the future – are the co-ordinates of the island on which we live. As an epigraph for his play Shepard chooses the words of Cesar Vallejo: 'Something identifies you with the one who leaves you, and it is your common power to return: thus your greatest sorrow. Something separates you from the one who remains with you, and it is your common slavery to depart: thus your meagerest rejoicing.' Between that going away and that remaining, the map of Ireland is stretched.

Shepard's image is more than fiction. The Irish folklorist Seamus O Catháin, working in a farming community in Wisconsin, met a woman who told him a story. When she was a girl, a neighbour of hers had a single word written on the side of his barn. To her, the word was a dumb hieroglyph, letters and shapes without meaning. It had no known connotation or significance. Years later, when she was a grown woman, she came to Ireland on a visit. There, by chance, she came across the word again – BELMULLET – and realised for the first time that it was a place name. It had stood on the side of that Wisconsin barn, a word without a meaning, a signifier in search of a signified, a place name without a place. Only now did it take on a content.

Such shadow place names are part of the Irish map. The poet Ciaran Carson came across another in New York: 'On an almost blank wall where East 46th Street intersects Avenue A in the area called Alphabet City in New York, New York, is the grafitto in three-foot-high black letters, saying BELFAST, with the cross-stroke of the T extended into an arrow pointing east, to Belfast. I have a photograph to prove this, but it's lost. In New York, no one that I ask seems to know the meaning of this careful scrawl, whether it's a gang, the code word of a gang, a fashion, a club, or the name of the city where I was born; but the latter seems unlikely, though Alphabet City – barricaded liquor stores, secretive tobacco shops and elaborate Russian

Orthodox churches – resembles Belfast, its roads pocked and skid-marked, littered with broken glass and crushed beer cans.'

3.

In the Tipperary Inn in Montauk, Long Island, there are three maps of Ireland on the walls. None of them gives you much of a guide to the present geography of the place. One of them is a 50-year-old map of a place called Eire, a schoolroom diagram in pastel colours of the mountain ranges and rivers that we learned off by heart and carried around in our heads like irregular verbs from an obscure and half-forgotten language. The second is a map of Literary Ireland. By definition, it is the map of a series of inventions, the places of writers, though if you know how to read it it may reveal something, since a map of the birthplaces of historic writers is also a map of absences, of places that these writers left behind.

The third map is still more fictional: a Genealogical Map of Ireland, its territories defined by the homes of tribes that were broken centuries ago, its borders decorated by the absurd crests and coats-of-arms that they borrowed from their conquerors centuries later in order to convince themselves that they had not, after all, been broken.

If none of these maps gives you much sense of direction, neither does the green street sign that hangs by the door: 'Sraid Aonrai/Henry Street'. In this context, Henry Street, that Dublin tunnel of cheeky charlies and wrapping paper, might be the name of a famous Irishman, or even a famous American. Hanging from the ceiling are three golden letters that are all that remains of what was once a banner: HAP ... Happy Birthday? Happy Thanksgiving? Happy Saint Patrick's Day? The Ireland that is being celebrated here is a bit like that banner: the tattered remains of something that must have been wonderful if anyone could remember what it was.

The clock in the Tipperary Inn is entirely innocent of the right time, but it is getting very late. Shuffling around the dancefloor to the sound of a band playing sixties hits are a few tanned American holiday-makers. They have spent the day pretending to be Ernest Hemingway, hunting striped bass or vast tuna fish from the charter boats, and now they want a few beers and a stretch on the floor. Yet, if you're Irish there is something surreal about the way Ireland, or a version of Ireland, can be a holiday destination even in New York State. You can visit a little bit of Ireland without ever leaving America.

What is even more surreal is that you visit America without ever really leaving Ireland. Every shop, every bar, every hotel in Montauk seems to be staffed by young Irish people. You walk in feeling hip in your shades and shorts, only to be asked in familiar tones: 'What's the weather like at home?' You have to think for a moment where home might be when a whole generation seems to be over here. There are so many Irish over here that that they have their own acronyms: as well as Yuppies and Dinkies, there are Biffos – Big Ignorant Fuckers From Offaly.

Anyway, it's very late in the Tipperary Inn, and the main entertainment is watching the last couple still on the dancefloor, him all muscles and shapes, her twice his age, done up to the nineteens, fretfully buying him drinks. It looks like it will soon be closing time.

Except that, for the Irish, it is now opening time. Bit by bit, they start to drift in, two or three at a time until the place is full again. They are all of an age – early to mid twenties – and they are all of a mind to enjoy themselves. You realise that, whereas for the tourists this is the fag-end of the day, for the Irish it is the beginning, the time when work has ended and the fun can start. The shops they work in have closed, the night staff have come on duty in the hotels. Soon the Americans will start to drift off to bed, leaving the place to the real natives, the people who work and make a life here, the Irish.

Not that this Irish life is settled. The tourist season is coming to a close and most of the Irish will have to move on, back to New York or Boston, or out West, or, if things are really slack, back to Mullingar and Dublin, Roscommon and Wexford. You meet the odd Irish person who works year-round on the fishing boats or the restaurants, but most are migratory emigrants, doubly unsettled, following the work. Tonight, some of the Irish have had a barbecue on the beach to say goodbye to each other. Their temporary communities resolve and dissolve themselves. Yet in the shifting, permanently temporary society of America, this is no big deal. The Irish here still seem like the consistent presence around which things revolve, the natives who have things better sussed, who know the ins and outs. These emigrants seem to define the place.

And some of them, the lucky ones who have Green Cards and university degrees, will become more and more settled with time. The wedding has now replaced the wake as the symbol of the permanence of emigration. Before, the American Wake, held on the night before the journey to Cobh for the boat, was the recognition that the emigrant was passing away to another side, probably for ever. You still meet older Irish immigrants in America who talk about 'the other side', meaning Ireland, as if emigration were a passage through the borders between one state of existence and another. But for the younger generation, who went to America young, free and single, it is the act of marrying in America that now marks the real passage to the other side, the final statement that home is no longer a place that you visit at Christmas time, but the place in which you put up the Christmas tree for your children.

To settle down is also to settle accounts, to draw a line under the transaction called 'Ireland', accept the losses and gains, and begin to define yourself as American. It is preferable to the never-ending cycle of emigration and return, to the fate of having to shift your country with every boom and recession, which is becoming, for more and more people, the reality.

And so, on the dancefloor of the Tipperary Inn, under the

auspices of three fictional maps of Ireland, the standard courtship rituals of the young have a special edge. The vague possibilities that always hover around a dancefloor, the possibilities of permanent links being formed, of families and generations arising out of these madcap revels, of somebody, somewhere, having a memory that their grandparents met on this floor, seem poignantly distant. Because some of them are illegal aliens, because many have just marked their departure from this place, because their lives are cast on the waters of uncertainty, how could a glimmer of the future ever break through those dancing eyes? If this were Ireland, and not just a maze of untrustworthy maps, at this hour the barman would long ago have asked 'Have yis no homes to go to?' But it isn't and they haven't.

In a country where the places and their names will not stick together because the places and their people have not stuck together, maps have to be descriptions of the imagination, of memory and desire, as well as of physical terrain. The most potent Irish maps of recent years, those of the Aran Islands and the Burren by Tim Robinson, are records, not merely of topography, but of the people he met, the stories he was told, while making them. Of his Aran map, Robinson wrote that he 'tried to see Aran through variously informed eyes – and then, alone again, I have gone hunting for those rare places and times, the nodes at which the layers of experience touch and may be fused together. But I find that in a map such points and the energy that accomplishes such fusions ... can, at most, be invisible guides, benevolent ghosts, through the tangles of the explicit; they cannot themselves be shown or named.' This sense that a map-maker has that there are ghosts behind the explicit, that the recorded details of the map owe much to what cannot be named or acknowledged, seems the only spirit in which a map of Ireland is possible. When Belfast is a mysterious graffito on a New York wall and Belmullet an inarticulate jumble of letters on the side of a Wisconsin barn, hidden presences and charged absences must haunt the maps we make.

4.

The unsettling of a nation is an easy work, the settling is not.
– Vincent Gookin, *The Great Case of Transplantation in Ireland*, 1655

Emigration, all-embracing as it is, is not the only force that belies the map of Ireland. There is a sense in which even the points of the compass are no longer fixed in Irish experience. Ireland ought to be one of the most clearly defined of public spaces. It is a bounded entity if ever there was one: a small island at the outer limit of one continent, Europe, and facing, across thousands of miles of ocean, another, America. But this is a trick of the eye, an illusion which tantalises the reality of a place that is permeable, that on the one hand seems connected to too many conflicting loyalties of place and on the other seems to melt away into the sea, as if the coastline that surrounds the country were merely a thin membrane that lets in all the flotsam and jetsam of consumer culture and lets out a constant flow of people and capital. On the one hand, in the North, there is no agreement about what the political space is: the United Kingdom or a United Ireland? On the other, in the South, there is constant difficulty in maintaining a political space at all.

If you see a country as its people rather than its territory, then, far from being small and well-defined, Ireland has been, for at least 150 years, scattered, splintered, atomised like the windscreen of a crashed car. In 1990, the population of Ireland was about the same as it was in 1890 after decades of famine, violence and mass emigration. All the natural increase in the meantime had been lost to emigration. Ireland is a diaspora, and as such is both a real place and a remembered place, both the far west of Europe and the home back east of the Irish-American. Ireland is something that often happens elsewhere. And this is both a cause and a consequence of its sense of being an unstable place, a place all the time having to struggle to become a political entity. A cause because emigration makes the borders of the island permeable. A consequence because, when you grow up in a country which it is hard to imagine as a political entity, then equally it is hard to imagine a way in which you might help to change that place. Change becomes personal, not political: you change your location, not your society.

In such a place, neither internal boundaries nor external co-ordinates hold their meaning. Even the most unconscious of boundaries, the old county divisions, separating one political constituency and, more importantly, one county hurling or football team, from another, are often uneasy and artificial. One of the most rooted of Irish writers, one of the most certain of his sense of place, is John McGahern, yet he has this to say about his native Leitrim: 'Except for football and politics, the county divisions mean little to the people. For those who live on the Shannon, North Leitrim might as well be Cornwall. It is each single, enclosed locality that matters and everything that happens within it is of passionate interest to those who live there. Do you have any news, any news? But once that news crosses a certain boundary, eyes that a moment before were wild with curiosity will suddenly glaze. News no longer local is of no interest.' More and more the boundaries are private and familial rather than public and political.

On the mental map of Ireland now, unlike the mental map in *An Béal Bocht* where all directions are one, the compass tends to point in all directions at once. Geography is a politics as much as it is a science. For Northern Protestants, Britain is the mainland, as if Northern Ireland were the Isle of Man. For Northern Catholics, West Belfast, although it is in the east of the island, is part of the West, because the West, for over a century now, has been the symbol of the pure, Catholic, native Ireland, and West Belfast wants to belong to that symbolism. Donegal, which is at the northern boundary of the island, is in the South, because it is part of the Republic. In Dublin, North and South are not points on the compass but social categories, the Northside supposedly working-class, the Southside supposedly middle-class, that allow the embarrassing subject of class division to be alluded to without being openly acknowledged. Direction is a matter of psychological orientation. History, not geography, defines the space you inhabit.

These contortions of north and south are now matched, and to an extent bypassed, by the other shifting axis of east and west. In Irish nationalist mythology, the West was the locus of the real Ireland, and the goal of politics was to make the whole country as like the West as possible. In reality, though, the West was marginalised economically and culturally, poorer, less populous, more vulnerable to the loss of its people through emigration. And, in the Single European Market, this double association of the West with romantic aspirations and with actual marginality is catching up with the country as a whole.

It has become hard for Irish politicians to decide whether their country is East or West. Albert Reynolds, then Taoiseach, told the *Irish Times* in November 1992 that his ambition was 'to link the Americans with Europe and to make Ireland the bridgehead in that link from west to east'. A bridgehead is a fortified military position held on the enemy's side of a natural barrier. So Ireland becomes a piece of Europe captured by America, a piece of America captured by Europe. It becomes neither east nor west, but some kind of embattled border zone.

Or consider a map of Ireland in Europe from *Manager-Magazin*, a glossy German business publication, of March 1990. The heading on the map is 'Boom, Boom, Boom: European growth in the 1990s'. Central and western Europe are shown with new divisions to replace the old borders. A banana-shaped 'North–South axis' encloses an area from the English south through Holland and Belgium, south-western Germany, Switzerland and northern Italy. A new country called 'Sunbelt' runs from Lyon through the Côte d'Azur, Catalonia and the north-eastern corner of Spain. And a thick blue line to the west of the map, arcing gracefully to the west of Scotland but east of

Ireland, down through much of Wales and the West Country, through Britanny and the west of Spain, invents a new place called 'Atlantik-Peripherie'. The only full country in it is Ireland, coloured a bold grey-green as are southern Spain and Sardinia and the south of Italy. Though we do not know it, this is where we live now.

For what the West of Ireland was to the rest of the country, Ireland as a whole, North and South, now is to the rest of the European Union: a romantic but backward periphery. The majority of the population which lives on the eastern half of the island has been used to thinking of itself as East, not West. Now, in the context of the EU, it has to think of itself as West, not East. On the scale of Europe, most of the country is a western margin, what the German map calls 'the Atlantic periphery'. In the hard white light of Euro-economics, space and place lose their romance and are reduced to a set of unpromising figures. Using an index of accessibility to European markets, Ireland is defined as part of the outer periphery, the lowest in a five-category spatial classification. Its accessibility score, in which space is converted into money, is only 55 per cent of the average of all the regions of the EU. It is 21 per cent and 17 per cent respectively of the Rheinhessen-Pfalz and of London, which belong to the 'core'.

In this new understanding of public space, this new map, places are related to each other not by their proximity or by the fact that they form part of the same nation or state, but by the fact that they share the same degree of accessibility to markets. The outer periphery, to which Ireland belongs, is not a little island but the 40 per cent of the land area of the EU that has just 20 per cent of the population and 13 per cent of the Gross Domestic Product. Distance is economic, not physical: Edinburgh may be as far from the Rhine as Dublin is, but it is part of the core, whereas Dublin is part of the outer periphery, simply because Edinburgh is more accessible and richer. In this sense, the new map of post-1992 Europe is one in which Dublin, and Belfast, are in the West, along with Warsaw, Bucharest and Lisbon, while Edinburgh and London are in the East along with Stuttgart and Nice and Rome. Where space is measured, not in miles or kilometres, but in marks or francs, it is hard to get your bearings.

It was, after all, another Irishman, Jonathan Swift, who invented in *Gulliver's Travels* the idea of a flying island, Laputa. Ireland is now a sort of flying island, hovering between a number of different contexts, often flying blind with no one too sure of how the controls work any more. It touches down now in the Bronx, now in Bonn, now in Britain, seeking connections with a set of overlapping places, but always taking off again into its own outer spaces.

5.

The word-world of Finnegans Wake has its own geography, and a very queer geography it is too, since it violates the geographical postulate of identification by fixed co-ordinates. Not only do the boundaries of Dublin expand to include the rest of the terrestrial globe and the indefinite loci of fiction and mythology, but the very dimensions of space itself become uncertainly elastic and transform themselves into one or more dimensions of time.
– Louis O. Mink, *A Finnegans Wake Gazetteer*

The geography of Ireland at the end of the twentieth century is a version of the queer geography of Joyce's *Finnegans Wake*, in which Dublin is also the Dublin that is the county seat of Laurens County, Georgia; Baile Atha Cliath is also Balaclava; Dublin is also Lublin; the New Ireland is the New Island (America); Crumlin is the Kremlin; West Munster is Westminister, and the four provinces are the erogenous zones of 'used her, mused her, licksed her and cuddled'. Its proper maps are those searched for by the great cartographer Tim Robinson, seeking those 'nodes at which the layers of experience touch and may be fused together'.

They may be nothing more than the map in Miroslav Holub's poem *Brief Thoughts on Maps*. According to the poem, a young lieutenant in a Hungarian regiment during the First World War sent a reconnaissance unit out into the icy wastes of the Alps. Almost immediately they were engulfed in a blizzard and lost from view. When they had not returned for two days, the lieutenant, racked with guilt, realised that he had sent his own people to their deaths.

On the third day, however, the reconnaissance unit came back. They admitted that they had lost their way and that, in despair, they had slumped into the snow to await the end. Then, on a final check, one of them had found a map in his pocket. That calmed them down and gave them heart. They pitched camp, waited out the snowstorm, and then, with the map, found their bearings. And here they were. The lieutenant borrowed the map, and had a good look at it. It was a map, not of the Alps, but of the Pyrenees.

1995

Going Native

The Irish as Black as Indians

'It was terrible weather too,' said the policeman, 'the day a nun found the dead Redskin on Duke Street ... No one ever found out where he came from, who he belonged to, no poison was found in him nor any sign of violence on him: he was clutching his tomahawk, he was in war paint and all his war finery, and since he had to have a name – we never found out what his real name was – we called him "our dear red brother from the air". "He's an angel", wept the nun – she wouldn't leave his side – "he must be an angel; just look at his face ..."'
– Heinrich Boll, *Irish Journal*, 1957

In October 1992, in the grounds of the community centre in Killinkeere, County Cavan, near the Irish border, a tree was planted in a ceremony of reconciliation. It was not, as might be supposed, a gesture of reconciliation between Protestants and Catholics, but between the Irish and the Indians. Killinkeere is the reputed birthplace of General Philip Sheridan, the American general who coined the phrase 'the only good Indian is a dead Indian'. A plaque on a house up a quiet lane on the road to Bailieboro, placed there by the American army, records the origins of the great Indian killer. Up that road, after more than a century, came a Native American woman, Joanne Tall from South Dakota, with her daughter ReaAnn, Oglala Sioux and descendants of Chief Crazy Horse. She came to reconcile this strange fact of Irish history, to plant a weeping willow and to exorcise a painful past. It stands there now amidst the fields, small but growing, an odd, inscrutible symbol of an unfamiliar Ireland, an Ireland nevertheless that makes more sense in the 1990s than many other versions of the place.

'Your music,' says Jimmy Rabbitte in the most popular Irish novel of recent years, Roddy Doyle's *The Commitments*, 'should be about where you're from and the sort of people you come from.' Nothing there, in essence, that could not have been said by Yeats or Synge or Lady Gregory, all of whom believed that a culture should be about the place and the people you come from. It's the bit that comes next that they might have had difficulty with: '"Say it once, say it loud, I'm black and I'm proud." They looked at him. "James Brown . . ." They were stunned by what came next. "The Irish are the niggers of Europe, lads." They nearly gasped, it was so true. "An' Dubliners are the niggers of Ireland . . . An' the Northside Dubliners are the niggers of Dublin – Say it loud I'm black an' I'm proud."'

How did we get from the beginning of that passage to the end, from Yeats to James Brown, from the idea of national cultural distinctiveness to the desire not just to be somebody else, but to be a different race, and an oppressed one at that? And why do you find, in works by younger Irish writers from urban communities, conscious usage of imagery linking the Irish not just to the blacks but to the Indians, a linkage that is sometimes playful and comic, but sometimes serious and almost literal.

Why, for instance, is perhaps the most accomplished play by any of the younger generation of Irish playwrights, Sebastian Barry's *White Woman Street*, an epic of the Wild West in which the Irish hero is haunted by the death of a young prostitute who was sold as being white but was really an Indian? Why in one of the most powerful Irish theatrical events of the 1990s, Druid's production of Vincent Woods's *At the Black Pig's Dyke*, do Leitrim mummers appear at times as Indian war-dancers? Why is the first published story of one of the most accomplished young novelists, Joe O'Connor's *The Last of the Mohicans*, an ironic play on the romance of the Indians? Why, in other words, is one of the characteristics of the new urban literature emerging in Ireland a desire to play with being black or Indian? This is an odd question, and to attempt to answer it requires a long diversion into the place from which urbanised Ireland takes its shapes, America.

In his great history of the Indian Wars of the eighteenth century, *The Conspiracy of Pontiac* (published in 1851), the American historian Francis Parkman makes a curious, unexplained connection in which a Frenchman who intermarries with the Indians becomes an Irishman, or at least a Celt. With all the disdain of the Boston brahmin for the compromise between civilisation and barbarism, Parkman sketches out the nightmare of cultivated society going native, of the forest encroaching on the town:

'From the beginning, the French showed a tendency to amalgamate with the forest tribes ... At first, great hopes were entertained that, by the mingling of French and Indians, the latter would be won over to civilisation and the church; but the effect was precisely the reverse; for, as Charlevoix observes, the savages did not become French, but the French became savages. Hundreds betook themselves to the forest, nevermore to return. These outflowings of French civilisation were merged in the waste of barbarism, as a river is lost in the sands of the desert. The wandering Frenchman chose a wife or a concubine among his Indian friends; and, in a few generations, scarcely a tribe of the west was free from an infusion of Celtic blood.'

The use of the adjective 'Celtic' in this vision of an Eden tarnished by original sin is strange but significant. The French would not generally be regarded as Celts, and, given that Parkman's book was written in Boston at the height of 'native' (i.e. WASP) American hysteria about the arrival of the Famine Irish, it is not hard to guess at the real source of his fear and disgust. The wild, ill-clad, superstitious savages, who might

20

swamp civilisation with their barbarism, mixing native and Celtic blood, were heeling up every day in Boston harbour.

In the course of his epic history, Parkman makes the image of the Celt, and specifically the Irishman as the locus of impurity, the dread crossroads at which civilisation and barbarism meet, more explicit. He writes with some fascination of the figure of Sir William Johnson, 'a young Irishman' who went to America in 1734 and gained a huge tract of land in New York state. Johnson was the major-general who commanded the English forces against the French at the Battle of Lake George. He was also superintendent of Indian affairs. His mistress, known as Molly Brant, was the sister of the Iroquois war chief. As a letter of Johnson's from 1765 shows, he also dressed and behaved like an Indian, or, as he put it more delicately to the Board of Trade, 'I was called to the management of these people, as my situation, and opinion that it might become one day of service to the public, had induced me to cultivate a particular intimacy with these people, and even to their dress on many occasions.'

When the American War of Independence was beginning to break out, Johnson, Irishman, subject of the English king, and brother to an Iroquois war chief, was faced with a terrible dilemma. If he remained loyal to the king, he would be required to lead his Indian army against his fellow American settlers. To be a proper white man, to prove his loyalty as the king's general, he would have to set the barbarians on the civilised people. In what Parkman calls an 'agony of indecision', he went mad and died suddenly, reputedly by his own hand. At the birth of the modern world, a now forgotten Irishman was plunged, by the impossible ambivalences of Irishness, caught between barbarism and civilisation, into madness and death.

Johnson's death as the modern world was entering its most decisive act of emergence, the birth of America, had a history and a culture. For Puritan civilisation, the plantation of Ireland and the contemporaneous plantation of America were inextricable. Christopher Hill, Oliver Cromwell's biographer, tells us that 'we should see Cromwell's Irish policy as part of his general imperial policy. The native Irish were treated much as the original settlers of New England treated the Indians. Cromwell wrote to New England to try to persuade "godly people and ministers" to move to Ireland.' Presumably their experience of civilising the Indians would come in handy with the Irish.

The Puritans had an ambivalence about plantation which derived from the fear of contamination and degeneracy. John Owen preached in 1685 that 'we are like a plantation of men carried into a foreign country. In a short space they degenerate from the manners of the people from whence they came and fall into that of the country whereunto they are brought.' The only plantation of which Owen had first-hand experience was Ireland, which is obviously the source of his image.

Francis Hutcheson in his *Inquiry into the Origin of our Ideas of Beauty and Virtue* (1725), itself a formative influence on the American revolution, remarks sardonically on 'the horror and admiration of the wondrous barbarity of the Indians, in nations no stranger to the massacre at Paris, the Irish rebellion, or the journals of the Inquisition', a phrase in which the violence of Catholics against Protestants, among them the Irish Catholic rebels, is explicitly linked to that of the Indians.

In America, the link between the Irish massacres of Protestants and the massacre of Indians became explicit in a supremely ironic way. In 1764, when Irish Presbyterians massacred the Contestoga Indians, they were accused of savagery by the Quakers of Philadelphia. A contemporary letter notes that 'the Presbyterians, who are the most numerous, I imagine, of any denomination in the province, are enraged with their being charged in bulk with these facts, under the name of Scotch-Irish, and other ill-natured titles, and that the killing of the Contestoga Indians is compared to the Irish massacres, and reckoned the most barbarous of either'.

The Quakers of Philadelphia gave the Indians shelter and the Irish backwoodsmen marched on the city, which had to be barricaded. For a brief moment, in the New World, the Irish were the Indians outside the walls of the civilised city. The Indians and the Quakers were the civilians inside. In this state, though they were Ulster Presbyterians, they could only be thought of by the defenders of Philadelphia as Irish papists. A satiric poem circulated by the Quakers inside the city pictured the leader of the Presbyterian attackers as an archetypal Irish papist:

> *O'Hara mounted on his Steed,*
> *Descendant of that self-same Ass,*
> *(That bore his Grandsire Hudibras,)*
> *And from that same exalted station,*
> *Pronounced an hortory oration:*
> *. . . 'Dear Sirs, a while since*
> *Ye know as how an Indian Rabble*
> *With practices unwarrantable,*
> *Did come upon our quiet Borders,*
> *And there commit most desperate murders . . .'*
> *He paused, as Orators are used,*
> *And from his pocket quick produced*
> *A friendly vase well stor'd and fill'd*
> *With good old wiskey twice distill'd,*
> *And having refreshed his inward man,*
> *Went on with his harangue again.*

The bluster, the whiskey, the absurd self-importance – all of the classic stereotypes of the Irishman are present, even in the view taken by one white Protestant of another. What matters is that the Irishman, in his slaughter of the Indians, has become himself a savage. He is, both literally and metaphorically, outside of the bounds of civilisation.

It is important to remember that this myth of the Celtic Indian was no mere momentary invention. It had roots that went back as far as the colonisation itself, though principally in a Welsh, rather than Irish, form. As early as the thirteenth century, stories of the discovery of magical islands to the west by a Welsh seafarer Madoc circulated in Europe. The Elizabethan polymath Dr John Dee transmuted these stories into a Welsh discovery of America as a weapon against Spanish claims on the New World. In the mid eighteenth century, this myth resurfaced as the early Welsh settlers in America began to report the existence of Welsh-speaking Indians, the descendants of Madoc. Scores of people reported conversations in Welsh with Indians. Several Indian chiefs swore to their Welsh ancestry. Many men told tales of having their lives saved by talking in Welsh to their Indian captors. At least thirteen real tribes were identified as Madoc's descendants and a further eight invented for the purpose. By the end of the eighteenth century, Madoc fever was raging all over the USA and belief in these Celtic Indians was almost universal. Indeed, much of the most important early exploration of the western frontiers was carried out in search of Welsh Indians.

Out of this strange dialectic of civilisation and barbarism, came the possibility of real Celts identifying themselves as Indians. In 1800–01, a virtual civil war in parts of Maine was conducted between the landed proprietors, chiefly General Henry Knox, on the one hand, and the so-called White Indians on the other. The White Indians were the European poor who had settled in the forests, chief among them the Irish. These were the kind of backcountry squatters of whom A. J. Dallas, a New York landlords' lawyer, complained in 1808: 'The Indians have hardly withdrawn from the ground and they are succeeded by a population almost as rude and as ferocious as themselves, coming for the most part from countries where the poor know nothing of the blessings of property and care little about its rights.' Ireland, of course, was pre-eminent among such countries.

The Maine backwoodsmen were largely Ulster Irish living in the forests around the settlement of Belfast. In July 1800,

General Knox's surveyors were ambushed by backwoodsmen 'blacked and disguised like Indians' and three were wounded. A year later, with the skirmishes continuing in the meantime, the backwoodsmen marched on the settlement of Belfast, 'dressed in Indian stile and perfectly black', making more explicit the dynamic of the march on Philadelphia in 1764: the White Indians outside the town, the civilised whites inside. Except that this time, the backwoodsmen were identifying themselves as Indians rather than setting out to slaughter Indians.

What we see in this shift is the emergence of the doubleness of the Celtic Irishman in racial imagery, the possibility that the identification with barbarism, black or Indian, can be a racial slur, or, alternatively, a badge of defiance. In the 'scientific' discourse on race which dominated so much of post-Darwinist debate in Britain, this doubleness is taken to the extreme of assuming that there were White Celts and Black Celts. The great Darwinian Thomas Huxley, even in defending the Irish against racial slurs, speculated on the existence of Black Celts: 'I am unaware of the existence of a dark-complexioned people speaking a Celtic dialect outside of Britannia (Ireland). But it is quite certain that in the time of Tacitus, the Silures, who inhabited South Wales and Shropshire, were a dark-complexioned people; and if Irish tradition is to be trusted for anything, we must credit its invariable assertion that only the chief Irish tribes – that of the Milesians – consisted of dark-haired, black-eyed people . . . In Ireland, as in Britain, the dark stock predominates in the west and south, the fair in the east and north . . . I believe it is this Iberian blood which is the source of the so-called black Celts in Ireland and in Britain.'

Given that the Irish, racially, can be regarded as black or white or anything in between in the nineteenth century, it is not surprising that non-Irish writers kept up their casual identification of the Irish with the Indians, and that, sometimes, the Irish chose to turn this intended slur into a badge of pride.

We find, for instance, Parkman in 1851 describing the

behaviour of Indian women in grief: 'All day they ran wailing through the camp; and when night came, the hills and woods resounded with their dreary lamentations ... The outcries of the squaws on such occasions would put to shame an Irish death howl.'

But this sort of imagery depends on its source, on the distinction between city and forest, on the fear of degeneracy which the intermixing of races would bring, on the contrast between civilisation and barbarism which the divide between town and forest or city and wilderness implies. What happens when there is no such distinction, when the Irish become urbanised? This happened in America long before it happened in Ireland, since the Irish in the nineteenth century urbanised themselves, not in Ireland, but in the great cities of America and Britain.

What happened is that the identification of Irish and Indian, set free of its moorings in fear of the forest, became playful, theatrical and a badge of pride. The same did not happen in relation to identification of Irish and blacks, because, after all, there were real blacks in New York and Chicago, and the Irish were often in direct competition with them. Two instances of this theatricalisation, the aestheticisation of the image of the Irish savage, can be mentioned. The first is in relation to Buffalo Bill Cody, whose Wild West shows were the medium through which the Indians became a commodified image. Cody's Irish ancestry was probably fairly distant, but it is important enough in the making of his showbusiness legend to be placed, in a comically exaggerated form, at the very beginning of the 1899 official family biography of Buffalo Bill by his sister Helen Cody Wetmore:

'The following genealogical sketch was compiled in 1897. The crest is copied from John Rooney's *Genealogical History of Irish Families*. It is not generally known that genuine royal blood courses in Colonel Cody's veins. He is a lineal descendant of Milesius, King of Spain, that famous monarch whose three sons, Heber, Heremon and Ir, founded the first dynasty in Ireland, about the beginning of the Christian era. The Cody family comes through the line of Heremon. The original name was Tireach, which signifies "The Rocks". Muireadach Tireach, one of the first of the line, and son of Fiacha Straivetine, was crowned king of Ireland, Anno Domini 320. Another of the line became king of Connaught, Anno Domini 701. The possessions of the Sept were located in the present counties of Clare, Galway and Mayo. The names Connaught-Galway, after centuries, gradually contracted to Connallway, Connellway, Connelly, Conly, Cory, Coddy, Coidy, and Cody, and is clearly shown by ancient indentures still traceable among existing records.'

Note in particular how close the racial ideology is to that already referred to in Huxley's consideration of Black and Iberian Celts. Note also that it is regarded as the essential beginning of the life of the man who was able to slaughter real Indians and then turn their image into a powerful international commodity.

The second aspect of this urbanised use of the identity of Irish and Indian is that most powerful Irish institution in the nineteenth and early twentieth centuries, Tammany Hall in New York. Tammany Hall was the political institution through which the Irish controlled the politics of New York for decades. It was named after the seventeenth century chief of the Delaware Indians, and its twelve leaders were called Sachems (the Indian word for chiefs) headed by the Grand Sachem. On Tammany Day, May 12th, it held a parade with hundreds of 'braves' marching through the streets with painted faces and carrying bows, arrows and tomahawks. When the Irish took over this institution, the White Indian had become not merely a gesture of backwoods protest, but a triumphant display of new urban power.

What was possible for the New York Irish at the turn of the century, however, was not possible for the Irish in Ireland at the same time, and did not become possible until they, too, began to develop a confidently urban self-image in the 1980s. In Ireland, at the turn of the century, the identification with blacks or Indians was still a real racial slur, still a tool of colonial oppression. The forest was real, not a literary metaphor. Rather than celebrate the White Indian or the Black Celt, they had to fend off the slur of racial impurity, of the notions of barbarism and degeneracy which went with it. The kind of Irishness which Buffalo Bill boasted about in his genealogy was impossible when Buffalo Bill's Wild West Show was being used, as in the report already quoted, as a horrible image of the inferiority of the Irish.

Instead, Irish literature set itself the task of inventing a counter-myth of national purity. Against the aestheticised celebration of impurity they set an insistence on the purity of the Gael, an image of the true Irish Gaelic peasant as the last remainder of an immemorial, untouched line. For the mainstream of Irish literature, the inherited categories were reversed. It was the city (i.e. England) which was degenerate, the wilderness which was pure. Parkman is turned on his head, but not in any way transcended. Canon Sheehan's novel *Luke Delmege* sums up the view of degeneracy when Fr Martin tells Luke: 'I never think of England but as in that dream of Piranesi – vast Gothic halls, machinery, pulleys, and all moving with the mighty, rolling mechanism that is crushing into a dead monotony all the beauty and picturesqueness of the world.' The countryside, meaning the Irish countryside, was the only true realm of authenticity and purity.

Yet this reversal was of no use to an emerging urban culture. Its need was not for an assertion of purity, which was anyway unsustainable in the context of a transatlantic culture as much influenced by Hollywood and the Rolling Stones as by the wood and stone of the Irish landscape, but for a way of celebrating impurity, of using the available aesthetic images of popular culture to speak about one's own society. For writers who grew up with Hollywood Westerns and black-inspired rock and roll music, Indians and blacks were available images that had both the texture of contemporary pop culture and an ironic subconscious prehistory in the most useful aspects of the Irish past, the Irish past that happened in America.

The availability of these images to Irish writers now does not depend on an appreciation of the more obscure corners of early American history. The White Indian is available in films such as John Ford's *The Searchers*, which is at one level about Ireland and America, but also in films which have nothing to do with Ireland, such as Werner Herzog's *Fitzcarraldo*, where the hero, played by Klaus Kinski, is an improbable Irishman, Brian Sweeny Fitzgerald, red hair and all, doing battle with the forest, in this case the Amazon rain forest. Somehow, when a dialectic of forest wilderness and urban civilisation is at stake, an Irishman is essential to the equation, even in a German film set in Amazonia. Think as well of Kipling's novel *Kim*, where the mediation between India and imperial Britain, between wilderness and empire, is carried on through the hero, an Irish boy named Kimball O'Hara. Or think in another context of Lawrence of Arabia, the most famous mediator between the Empire and the Arabs, and his fantasy that he was really the son of an Irishman, George Bernard Shaw.

In the emerging Ireland of the 1960s and after, the White Indian became a way of replacing history with irony, identity with a mongrel freedom, post-colonial angst with jokey doubleness. The new Tammany Hall politicians of 1960s Fianna Fáil – the up-coming generation of Charles Haughey, Brian Lenihan and Donough O'Malley – were dubbed 'The Mohawks' by their sceptical colleague Kevin Boland. Their attitude to the letter of the law was also distinctly Wild West, encapsulated in O'Malley's story of being caught driving the wrong way up a one-way street and of his reply to the policeman who caught him: 'See the arrows, guard? To tell the truth, guard, I didn't even see the bloody Indians.'

As with the Irish who strutted down the streets of New York in Indian garb to proclaim their new-found power, to celebrate the fact that the savages had conquered civilisation, the Indian metaphor has been taken on by contemporary Irish culture as a device which frees it from the burden of identity and lets it loose to play games with the world. The lost tribe of Celtic Indians has found a home on the range.

1993

Meanwhile Back at the Ranch

Images of Ireland and America

Here are three items of news from Ireland after the end of the 1980s:

Item 1: from the *Daily Star*, 30 January 1990. 'Gunslinger Clint Eastwood is descended from a Lord Mayor of Dublin . . . Clint, hero of the Dirty Harry movies, is believed to be descended from Alderman John Eastwood, mayor of Dublin in 1679. And Clint himself is a former mayor of the seaside town Carmel, in California. But his ancestor was also a sheriff of Dublin – on the opposite side of the fence to the stubble-jawed outlaw of the spaghetti westerns.'

A tentative conclusion from this news is that while all history is an invention, in Ireland the sense of the past is becoming an invented invention, refracted through the manufactured myths of the American movies. An Irish sheriff and a Wild West sheriff, the mayor of Dublin and the mayor of Carmel, California, 1679 and 1967, are all part of the same fiction, shooting it out on the main street of some eternal Tombstone.

Item 2: from *Magill*, February 1990. The first of Ireland's new commercial local radio stations to get into serious financial trouble is Radio West. It was established in Galway to the same formula and by the same people who ran a successful pirate station in Dublin called Treble-T R, playing the same diet of country and western music. But whereas the formula had found a ready audience with country people living in Dublin, it failed to appeal to country people living in the country. 'It may well be,' says the report, 'that a music policy which appealed to country people in flats in Dublin was to have much less appeal when directed at the same people on their home ground.'

A tentative conclusion from this news is that even the country and western culture imported into Ireland from America is itself an aspect not so much of modernity as of nostalgia, a part of the dynamics of memory and displacement, of exile and yearning. When Irish people yearn for America they may not yearn for an America of the present but an America of the past, a remembered America, a myth of America created by their own ancestors. The Irish country people in the city wanted to listen to country and western because it reminded them of their past, and that image of the past was American. The Irish country people living at home had less need for such nostalgia, for such an invented American past.

Item 3: from the *Sunday Tribune*, 25 February 1990. A film production company called Virginia Films is to hold the premiere this summer of their documentary *The Road to Inishfree* in Cong Town Hall, County Mayo. The film is a re-enactment of the filming of John Ford's *The Quiet Man* in Cong thirty-nine years ago. Locals Anne Slattery and Paul Kane were hired to play Maureen O'Hara and John Wayne, playing John Ford's film characters based on Maurice Walsh's fictional characters. '*The Road to Inishfree*', says the report, 'reconstructs selected moments from *The Quiet Man* including the famous bicycle scene.' Anne Slattery hasn't seen the final product and half expected never to see it. 'I shot my scenes almost two years ago but I haven't heard from the company since and I thought the film was shelved.' Another actress who played in the documentary says she won't be at the premiere because she has since emigrated.

A tentative conclusion from this news is that it is not so much the past that we re-enact in Ireland but an American movie version of the past. We play out a dramatised version of someone's else's dramatised version of ourselves, a drama which the actors never expect to be finished, or, if it is finished, cannot expect to be around to see.

What I want to suggest is that America and Ireland represent not opposites, not a dialogue of modernity and tradition, but a continual intertwining in which, far from Ireland being the past and America being the future, America can constitute Ireland's past and Ireland can invent America's future. When we deal with this relationship, we are dealing not with something final and closed, but with something obsessive, repetitive, continually unfinished, all the time renewing itself in old ways. We are dealing with the schizophrenic dynamics of memory and exile. And exile is both *from* and *to*. It is about both leaving and returning. In the imaginative geography of exile, everything is relative to everything else. The West of Ireland is West for Ireland, East for America. The American West can take on the contours of the Ireland back home, back east. I want to try and suggest some ways in which the notion of America itself is an Irish invention, the notion of Ireland an American invention. When we step into this divide, we step into, not an open space, but a hall of mirrors.

The first important contradiction that I want to explore in this dynamic of exile is that between the native and the civilised. The American myth, of course, is the myth of the taming of the wilderness, the conquering of the uncivilised Indian by the civilised white man. The Irish, of course, played more than their fair part in this process. But the ambivalence comes from the fact that the Irish are not, in this dichotomy, either/or, they are both/and. They are natives and conquerors, aboriginals and civilisers, a savage tribe in one context, a superior race in another. At the same time as the West of America is being opened up, British colonial language is using the savagery of the Indian tribes as a convenient analogue for the native Irish. In 1844, an English traveller in Ireland remarks that 'The murders of this country would disgrace the most gloomy wilds of the

most savage tribes that ever roamed in Asia, Africa, or America.'
In 1865 an editorial in the *London Times* links the genocide of
the American Indian with the genocide of the Irish, in a spirit of
glee rather than outrage: 'A Catholic Celt will soon be as rare
on the banks of the Shannon as a Red Indian on the shores of
the Manhattan.' As the language of the Wild West and the
Indian Wars becomes generalised through popular fiction and
journalism – the one generally indistinguishable from the other
– it becomes easy to apply this language to the wild Irish. A
British visitor looking at Tuam in County Galway late in the
last century thinks immediately of the Red Indians: 'Not only
are the cabins in this district aboriginal in build but they are
also indescribably filthy and the conditions of the inmates . . . is
no whit higher than that obtaining in the wigwams of the native
Americans. The hooded women, black-haired and bare footed,
bronzed and tanned by constant exposure, are wonderfully like
the squaws brought from the Far West by Buffalo Bill.' *Punch*
talks of 'a tribe of Irish savages, the lowest species of the Irish
yahoo'. For Britain, the Irish are the Indians to the far west,
circling the wagons of imperial civilisation.

Once in America, of course, the Irish cease to be the Indians
and become the cowboys. They are the Indian killers and the
clearers of the wilderness. They are the mythic cowboys. Jesse
James's father comes from Kerry; Billy the Kid, though known
eventually as William Bonney, is initially known as Henry
McCarty, son of Catherine McCarty. According to some contemporary reports he was born in Ireland, according to others
New York, and the ambivalence itself is perfect. In his legend as
it grows up he is a prodigious killer of Indians. He kills three
Apaches in Sonora, rescues Texans from Apaches with the
James gang. He takes on twenty 'well armed savages' in the
Guadelupe Mountains with only his six-gun and his dirk. But in
reality, or as much of reality as there ever can be in this kind of
legendary terrain, Billy the Kid fought not Indians but Irishmen.
In the Lincoln County Wars he fought against the Murphy-

Dolan-Riley ranching combine. The first murder he was charged with was that of the Murphy-Dolan-Riley sheriff, William Brady, a fellow Irish-American. And, of course, Billy himself was killed by another Irish-American, Pat Garrett. In this seminal American myth the struggle of Irishman with Irishman in the New World is transmuted into a struggle of white man against native. Billy the Kid is Irish and American. His victims are Irish and Indian. The Irish are the killers and the victims, the civilisers and the wild men, the good guys and the bad guys. An important part of the American psyche, the ambivalence of the desperado as dangerous outlaw and rugged individualist, arises out of the ambivalence of the Irish in America. This is Ireland inventing America. And the Billy the Kid myth is itself crucially ambivalent. The transformation of Billy from foot soldier in an economic war into hero of the war against the Indians is an acceptance of the Irish as part of the governing American myth. But the ease with which Billy's Irish antagonists can become Indian antagonists shows how close the Irish remain to the Indians in the 'civilised' mind. This tension between acceptance and exile, between being insiders and outsiders, liberates a set of images that is enormously influential on the development of American culture and therefore on the development of Irish culture.

This set of images is one which emerges always in a curiously self-referential way. It is not just in modern Ireland that the relationship with America is conducted through life-imitating-art-imitating-life. This is a feature of the Irish-American cultural construct right from the start. The whole myth of the American West is one in which life and art imitate each other with dizzying speed. Buffalo Bill's Wild West Show has cowboys and Indians re-enacting their wars as theatre almost as soon as they have ceased to be wars. Far from being the originator of a myth, Billy the Kid himself grew up in the mythological shadow of Jesse James. Theatricality, Irishness and the Wild West intertwine with abandon in the James story.

According to the legend, Jesse rode into the town of St Joseph on Saint Patrick's Day 1882 to lead the Saint Patrick's Day Parade on a stallion with green ribbons braided into its mane and tail. A month later an Irish playwright, one Oscar Wilde, was in the same town in Missouri on his American tour. He wrote in a letter from there that 'Outside my window about a quarter mile to the west stands a little yellow house and a crowd of people are pulling it all down. It is the house of the great train robber and murderer, Jesse James, who was shot by his pal last week, and the people are relic hunters. They sold his dustbin and foot scraper yesterday by public auction, his doorknocker is to be offered for sale this afternoon, the reserve price being about the income of an English bishop.' The pal whom Wilde mentions, Bob Ford, the Irishman who killed Jesse, then took a job with the repertory companies who were playing dramas about the James Boys, appearing at the interval to tell the story of how he shot Jesse. Jesse's brother Frank, meanwhile, got a job in another theatre company playing a cowboy in Wild West shows.

That this nexus of strange connections between showbusiness, Irishness and the Wild West is not merely an exotic aspect of frontier history becomes clear when you start to look at the way it enters American high culture in the work of Eugene O'Neill, and continues through American popular culture in the work of John Ford. The meaning of this self-conscious and intricate theatricality is the meaning of exile itself. Exile is a form of self-dramatisation, the assumption of a role, the tailoring of one's personality to an alien audience. Exile makes things that are unconscious – language, gesture, the accoutrements of nationality – conscious. It makes the exile a performer. And that performance involves ambiguity. It involves being who you are and being who you are playing. It involves, for the Irish in America, playing the white man and remembering the Indian that is left behind. And so, the notion of play-acting itself becomes an inextricable part of the Irish ambivalence, an essential image of the doubleness of the exile's condition.

Thus it is with Eugene O'Neill. In *Long Day's Journey Into Night*, O'Neill embodies Ireland as an actor, James Tyrone. Tyrone's pull between his Irish past and his American present is also a pull between life and performance, between being who he is and playing who he should be in order to be accepted in America. It is a pull between being the Indian and playing the cowboy, between his son's description of him as an Irish bog-trotter and his own belief that Shakespeare and the Duke of Wellington were Irish Catholics. And the same is true of Cornelius Melody in *A Touch of the Poet*, forever performing like an Irish Catholic combination of Shakespeare and the Duke of Wellington, dramatising himself in his military redcoat. 'Ain't he the lunatic,' remarks O'Dowd, 'sittin' like a play-actor in his red coat, lyin' about his battles with the French.' Both Tyrone and Melody are members of the savage Irish tribe appropriating the culture and the conquests of the white man. They are half-Indian, half-white man, and that division is their tragedy.

The connection between O'Neill and Billy the Kid may not be obvious but it is worth remembering that there is a similar mechanism of assimilation and rejection at work in both cases. Billy the Kid is the wild Irish savage but also the rugged White American, and in the development of his legend this tension is eventually resolved by dealing with Billy in conjunction with his father, his direct Irish antecedent, and splitting one off from the other. In Walter Wood's 1903 play on Billy the Kid it is the Kid's father who is the villain and who gets killed in the end in mistake for his son. Billy lives on, and starts a new life 'where the sun always shines' in peaceful, civilised America. The savage Irish part is punished and expunged, the good American part is civilised and domesticated.

And something of the same mechanism is at work in both *Long Day's Journey* and *A Touch of the Poet*. It is the Irish father who is the problem, who is blighting the lives of his Irish-American children. It is the Indian savage inside the Irishman that threatens the happiness of his children. Tyrone's mixture of meanness and fantasy, Melody's helplessly selfish dreams. For inside the Irishman is the primitive tribesman trying to get out. It is the Irishman inside that stops Tyrone from acting generously towards his family. And in *A Touch of the Poet*, the Irishman inside actually gets out. A blow on the head makes Melody regress to primitive savage. His cultured voice changes back to the thick Irish brogue. His pretensions towards being a gentleman are dropped and he refers to his acquired American self in the third person, as someone else, a ghost, a dead man. All the biological pessimism in O'Neill, even in an early play like *The Hairy Ape* where it is not yet articulated in direct confrontation with the notion of Irishness, is to do with this sense of the primitive savage that lies inside the Irish-American attempt at sophistication. It is to do with the cowboy's fear that he might, after all, be just another Indian.

What is interesting about the way in which the Irish-American relationship works is that, having been put on the stage by a figure who is both Irish and American, this image becomes available to playwrights who are either Irish or American. On the one hand, in an Irish play, Thomas Kilroy's *Double Cross*, the British cabinet minister Brendan Bracken, born in Ireland but hiding his Irish background, is caught in an explosion and suddenly the primitive Irishman is given the chance to emerge, speaking again in a thick brogue: 'me father was wan of the lads, so he was, wan of the hillside men ... Bejasus I was. I knew the treason prisoners of sixty-five.'

And on the other hand, the image of the half-Indian half-cowboy is available to an American playwright like Sam Shepard. In a Shepard play like *True West* or his screenplay for *Paris, Texas*, the wild brother who comes out of the desert, Indian territory, confronts the civilised brother who is settled in American comfort. Interestingly in both cases, the settled brother is involved with the equivalent of James Tyrone's theatricality, in one case with the movies, in the other with advertising. But the two brothers are halves of one whole, the tribal Indian part coming to haunt the settled, civilised part. The story is not now Irish, but it has its origins in an Irish-American dynamic, in the place where Eugene O'Neill and Billy the Kid meet. And in his play *A Lie of the Mind*, Shepard acknowledges the Irish dimension of this American sense of doubleness. At the beginning of the third act of the play, Lorainne is remembering herself as a young girl dressed up in western outfits for dances, what she calls a 'big Frontier Days blowout'. She immediately starts to search on a map, but she is looking, not for the frontier, but for County Sligo. She finds it and holds up the big map of Ireland on the stage. She decides to go back, even though she has never been there and knows no one in the country. 'They'll know. All I gotta do is tell 'em my maiden name and they'll remember ... We'll just stay for a little visit. Save on motel bills.' There is, as I hope I've shown, a subterranean logic to this slide from the frontier days to County Sligo, from the American past to an invented Ireland.

Shepard's frequent use of the desert as the territory of the wild man, of social amnesia, of a force that underlies and undermines civilisation, is itself indebted to the work of another Irishman, John Ford. Of all the artists who shape this intricate relationship between Ireland and America, Ford is the most truly ambivalent. Brought up speaking Irish and English, moving as a child between the States and County Mayo, working in his films with an invented America and an invented Ireland, Ford both embodies and formulates the tensions. He creates both an acceptable fiction of what America is and an acceptable fiction of what Ireland is, and both, indistinguishably, help to mould Ireland's notion of a mythic America that is part of our own past, that belongs to us almost as a tradition or a heritage. Monument Valley and the Cong of *The Quiet Man* are equally aspects of Irish Romanticism, equally the invention of an Irish artist.

Ford's paradox is that he is at his most Irish in his American films, at his most American in his Irish films. *The Grapes of*

Wrath may be a quintessential piece of Americana, but it is also deeply influenced by the Irish Famine. The displacement that is at work in it – a simple family thrown off their land and forced westwards to confront a class society at work – is the displacement of the Famine Irish forced out of their land and westwards into a confrontation with a class society. *The Quiet Man*, on the other hand, may be a quintessential part of the Irish imaginative landscape, but it is a deeply American film, concerned with Ireland only as an aspect of the past. The hero of the film, Sean Thornton, is an exile from his native land, the United States, trying to establish a place for himself in a country that is unmistakably foreign. And this paradox is carried through even more profoundly into the very landscape of the films. As Joseph McBride and Michael Wilmington have put it, 'There is a strange irony involved in Ford's visual metaphors for Ireland, the land of his ancestors, and the (American) West, the land of his dreams. The rocky, starved soil, which so many people fled, is seen as a lush green endlessly fertile valley, and the American Dream to which they escaped is a desert valley, slashed intermittently by rivers which serve only to emphasise its essential aridity.' In this paradoxical manipulation of images, the American West becomes the West of Ireland, Ireland becomes the rich promised land of the American West. The dynamics of memory and exile are not denied, they are reversed.

For a time, Ford was able to use this juggling of East and West, the west of Ireland back east and the American west, to embody a kind of social optimism about the American dream. The Mayo of Ford's ancestry is both East and West – west of Ireland, east of America – and in a film like *My Darling Clementine* this ambivalence allows the coming together of East and West on a mythic level. The hero of the film, Wyatt Earp, achieves his mythic status by embodying the best values of East and West. He is both rugged and civilised, both the man who comes in from the desert and the man who imposes order on the wild territory, both the individualist and the bearer of authority. This important part of America's creation myth owes, through Ford, a great deal to Ireland.

But what is interesting is that this ideal unity cannot last, that within ten years of *My Darling Clementine*, it breaks down in Ford's work into the .pain, uncertainty and confusion of *The Searchers*. In *My Darling Clementine* Wyatt Earp is easily able to overcome the disruptive Indian who is one of his first conquests in Tombstone. But in *The Searchers* ten years later, Ethan Edwards (the John Wayne character) cannot so easily subdue the Indians because he carries the Indian inside him. The deft merging of Ireland and America in *My Darling Clementine* has become again the painful ambiguity of Eugene O'Neill, the cowboy who carries the Indian about within himself. Like a James Tyrone or a Cornelius Melody, Ethan Edwards is a man of American civilisation, the white settler community, who can never be part of that community because he retains a powerful affinity with the Indian, the savage tribesman. He has all the characteristics of a Western hero – strength, individualism, leadership ability, self-sufficiency – but he is at the same time anti-social, outlawed even. He is both hunting the Indians and intensely close to them, knowing their language, their signals, their meaning, sharing their instincts for violence and revenge. He is, in other words, the perfect image of the Irish in America, both Indian and Indian-killer. The film's emotional tension depends on the whole question of sexual relations between whites and Indians, of the mixing of white and Indian blood, and that mixture is intensely connected to the relationship of Ireland and America. And in *The Searchers* that relationship has become sour. In the end, Ethan Edwards comes to the door of the white folk's cabin but cannot be admitted. He must turn and go back out into the desert, into Indian territory. The American Dream reveals its aspects of nightmare.

And it is important, too, that Ford repeats another part of O'Neill's triple connection of Irishness, the Wild West and theatricality. Think, for instance, of what Ford does with Lady

41

Gregory's play *The Rising of the Moon* in his film version, made shortly after *The Searchers*. Whereas in the play, a rebel about to be executed is rescued by another rebel, in Ford's version the rebel is rescued by the actors of the Abbey Theatre. A play-acted version of reality is turned into a play-acted version of play-acting. We are definitely into the hall of mirrors, where an Irish theatrical version of Irish reality becomes an American film version of Irish theatre-as-reality and, when shown in Ireland, is accepted as more real than the original play might ever have been. The obsessive, pathological nature of these transformations is what makes Ford's Irish films so bad when compared to his American films. What he is about in the Irish films is trying to expunge Irish reality, to cut out the painful, ambiguous Ireland that the American Ford must carry around inside him by turning the real Ireland into a harmless fiction. In his films, Ford takes Irish fiction – O'Casey and O'Flaherty in particular – and reduces it, getting rid of the ambivalence of, say, *The Plough and the Stars* or *The Informer*, as if by reducing the ambivalence of Irish fiction the haunting ambivalence of Irish-American reality can be exorcised.

Ford's real Ireland is Monument Valley, the American desert landscape that has all the qualities of timelessness, freedom from history and social amnesia that the Irish Romantic movement always sought in the West of Ireland. The desert is the ultimate absence of civilisation and Ford's affinity with it is the ultimate extension of Ireland as uncivilised, free, timeless. The essential ambivalence of the desert lies in the fact that it is both wild, and therefore frightening, and at the same time an alternative wilderness to the wildness of the American city. Jean Baudrillard says that 'There is the same wildness in the endless, indifferent cities as in the intact silence of the Badlands ... Death Valley and Las Vegas are inseparable.' For the Irishman drawn to the cities of the New World but distrusting them as alien, the desert represents the perfect form of exile, wild like the cities but natural, indifferent like the cities, but splendidly so. In the cities and in Ford's Monument Valley everything human seems artificial, out of place. For the exile from Ireland, the desert is an acceptable kind of city and this is the source of its ambivalent power.

The essential Irishness of Ford's use of the desert helps at least in some measure to explain why the most powerful use of the desert in post-war western culture is that of an Irishman, Samuel Beckett, in whose work the desert becomes the image of the modern world, of the dislocated urban world that we inhabit. It helps to explain the way in which it is an Irish rock band, U2, who have been able to recreate Ford's mythic America largely through their use of the deserts of Colorado and Arizona as a dream landscape in their photographic images, their films *Under a Blood Red Sky* and *Rattle and Hum*, their carefully worked-out Wild West costuming, and their post-apocalyptic born-again lyrics which use the desert as the image of a world after the nuclear holocaust.

And at the same time, the sense of the affinity with the Indians remains in contemporary Irish culture. One of the most important Irish novels of recent years, Brian Moore's *Black Robe*, plays deftly on the Irish ambivalence about native and civiliser. The novel's point of view moves between the Catholic missionary sent to Christianise the heathen Indians and the Indians themselves, a split which reflects the continuing resonance in a North American setting of the Irish connection to both the white man and the Indian. Or think of Paul Muldoon's recent poem *Meeting the British*, in which the 'we' of the narrative voice are the Indians but given the poem's title and situation of a meeting between the natives and the invading British cannot but include the Irish. The metaphor, again, is of the Irish as Indians, and the fact that the metaphor can be used as in the poem self-consciously, ironically, playfully, suggests the strength of its provenance.

Even more striking is the way in which this connection between the Irish and the inhabitants of the desert can be used by an American writer with no Irish connections and even by the international media. Take, for example, Don DeLillo's 1971 *Americana*, a novel which very consciously revisits John Ford's territory of Monument Valley and its curious overlapping of a real and an imaginative landscape. In the screwed-up logic of the novel's narrator, there grows an identification between the West of Ireland and the desert-dweller, between the Aran Islands and the Sahara, between the Irishman and the modern equivalent of the Indian, the Arab. 'Now that history has absolved me, I think I'd like to go very far away – to the Aran Islands, to the Sahara, to some village high in the Himalayas. There to situate my stale body and well-paid mind against the wild dogs of nature. Sea, desert and mountain ... I spin my Harry Winston prayer wheel. Or I stand above the furious sea, urbane man of Aran, spitting in my own face ... Pure mathematics of the desert ... All secrets are contained in the desert. Lines intersecting the sand. Where you are and what you are. Bedouinism in all its bedpan humour. Buckmulliganism in its bowl. An Irish Arab lives in my inner ear, announcing news, weather and sport. He is Jesuit educated and wears the very best that dogma can buy.' The lines that intersect in this sand are lines drawn by O'Neill, by Ford, by the Irish internalisation of the Empire's view of us as squaws living in wigwams. And these are connections, however bizarre, that can be made with ease in modern culture. In 1982, for instance, the New Zealand *Truth* newspaper ran an editorial after IRA bombings in London which brought the same Irish Arabs into the annals of current affairs: 'While terrorism in any form, in any country, is appalling, there is something about the Irish band – like that of the PLO against Israel – that makes Irish (or Palestinian) nationality difficult to bear among civilised people.'

The Irish Arab replaces the Irish Indian, but still rides across the wild desert, far from civilised people. On a more benign level, and slightly less seriously, one might remark that Edward Said's recent reclaiming of Yeats as a great Palestinian poet in his Field Day pamphlet 'Nationalism, Colonialism and Literature' is a part of the same strange sequence of connections.

Meanwhile back at the ranch there is a real Ireland and a real America, places connected not so much by myth as by profit and loss, productive investment, decisions made in boardrooms in Pittsburgh that reverberate in Castlebar, real cowboys running the country and real Irish Indians serving burgers in fast food joints in the Bronx. What I've been trying to suggest here is that an imaginative connection between Ireland and America is not a simple question of a clash between a traditional and a modern culture, but a much more complex set of cross-fertilisations in which America's cultural sense of itself is partly an Irish creation and Ireland's sense of itself is partly an American creation. And that nexus of connections is an essentially nostalgic and mythic one, nostalgic because it is concerned with an old vision of the American past, with cowboys and Indians, mythic because it has nothing at all to do with life either in America or Ireland now. We need to get out from under that myth. We need to turn the mirrors into windows.

1990

The Ghost and the Machine

The Legacy of the Kennedys

1.

After the torch had been passed to a new generation, after his son had been sworn in as the thirty-fifth President of the United States, old Joe Kennedy went to the celebration lunch for his family which he had arranged at the Mayflower Hotel in Washington. He found a huge table in the buffet room, and hundreds of people milling around it. He had never seen most of them in his life before, and he was mightily annoyed. 'Who are these people?' he asked the social secretary who had organised the lunch. 'Your family, Mr Ambassador,' she replied. 'They are not. Just who are these freeloaders?' Old Joe grabbed the nearest half dozen guests and demanded to know their names. Sure enough, they were Kennedys and Kennedy in-laws, Bouviers and Fitzgeralds. 'They are all family,' Old Joe admitted, 'and it's the last time we get them all together too, if I have anything to say about it.' Meanwhile, down on the old stone quay in New Ross, County Wexford, they were lighting bonfires and brushing up on family connections.

When John F. Kennedy arrived at Dublin Airport thirty years ago, he conjured up an image of a broken scattered family being re-united. He stood on the tarmac, tanned and gleaming, and told us that 'No country in the world, in the history of the world, has endured the haemorrhage which this island endured over a period of a few years, for so many of its sons and daughters. These sons and daughters are scattered throughout the world, and they give this small island a family of millions upon millions who are scattered all over the globe.' In his words, in his presence, was the tacit promise that all of these sons and daughters and in-laws would be brought together again at the great buffet table of the post-war boom. But, in our hearts, we probably knew that when we arrived for the feast, we would still be confronted by a sour old man muttering 'Just who are these freeloaders?' and demanding that we reveal our names.

In retrospect, the ambivalence of that moment of arrival is striking. Even the image of family that was trotted out with such apparent comfort is disturbingly paradoxical. Eamon de Valera, President of Ireland, went to greet Kennedy at the airport and it was as if, here as well as in Washington, the torch was being passed to a new generation. There was a ceremonial, even ritual, air to the occasion, to this strange squaring of the circle. An Irish president born in Brooklyn came to do homage to an American president 'from' New Ross. And to this strange symmetry was added the aura of a ritual succession of kingship, for these two men could have been father and son, and we were swapping the monkish, puritanical image of Ireland which de Valera embodied for the smooth, sexy, urbane Kennedy.

The disturbing question, though, was who was the father and who the son? President de Valera spoke to President Kennedy now as a proud father, now as a humble and grateful child. In his address of welcome, he spoke to Kennedy like a beaming daddy who has called his boy into the study to congratulate him on his exam results. He called him 'a distinguished son of our race' and told him frankly, 'We are proud of you, Mr President.'

But at other times, he spoke like an awed child, or like the chief of a remote tribe who has just been presented with a looking-glass and a necklace of cheap beads by a captain of the Royal Navy who is all the while eyeing his island for signs of removable wealth. He greeted Kennedy, not as President of America, but as 'the first citizen of the great republic of the West, upon whose enlightened, wise and firm leadership hangs the hope of the world'. The great republic of the West – the great white kingdom beyond the sea whose leader offers the natives fatherly protection and in return asks only for breadfruit. Had it been *Mutiny on the Bounty*, Kennedy would then have been offered a war dance and a choice of the young girls.

This ambivalence, this strange mixture of homage and absurdity, continued whenever Kennedy mentioned de Valera. In his address to the combined houses of parliament, for instance, he said: 'If this nation had achieved its present political and economic stature a century ago, my great-grandfather might never have left New Ross, and I might, if fortunate, have been sitting down there among you. Of course, if your own president had never left Brooklyn, he might be standing up here instead of me.'

The words were ingratiating, and were obviously meant courteously, but the images they conjur up must, even then, have been comic and mocking: John F. Kennedy parliamentary secretary to the Minister for Local Government, answering questions about the state of the road between Ballina and Belmullet. Eamon de Valera and his lovely wife Jackie and their children Mick, Tadhg, Carmel and Concepta, having a quiet evening at the White House with their friends Marilyn Monroe and Frank Sinatra. It was a very big 'if', so big as to remind us all the more forcefully of our dowdy little place in the world.

The same 'if' was on Kennedy's lips when he spoke on New Ross quay about his great-grandfather: 'If he hadn't left, I'd be working over at the Albatross Company, or maybe for John V. Kelly.' The double-edge was cutting. On the one hand, every factory worker in New Ross could imagine himself, for an instant, as this tanned gorgeous man, radiating power and sex, and the thought, however instantaneous, could not be anything but pleasant. On the other hand, the instant after, the meaning of that sentence would clarify itself in the mind: 'If we Kennedys hadn't got the hell out of here, even I'd be a no-good schmuck like you.' Which would you rather be, the most powerful man in the world, or a member of John V. Kelly's loyal staff?

He went on, standing there on that quay, to tell a joke. It was the story of the New Ross man who emigrated to the States. He was doing alright, but not as well as emigrés have to pretend to be doing to the folks back home. So he went on a trip to Washington, and stood in front of the White House, and got a passer-by to take a picture of him. He sent the photograph back home, and written on the back were the words: 'This is our summer house. Come and see it.'

Did he know what he was doing, telling this story to us? Did he know that that was what all those photographs of his visit would be, a message to ourselves back home in our dreary lives, to pretend to ourselves that we were doing well? Did he know that the unwritten words on the backs of those photographs of our faces in the crowds, beaming at him in beatific bliss, pressing towards him as towards a messiah, were 'This is my cousin. He came to see me'? Was he savouring the secret triumph of his power, that he was inside the White House, while we, poor Paddys, were standing outside the railings concocting false images to hide our failures?

He was a good actor, a star performer. He knew tricks that we were too naïve, too excited, too grateful, to see through. There was one particular trick that he used again and again on his visit here, and that we fell for every time, like the suckers we so badly wanted to be. He did it first in Cork, while he was accepting the freedom of the city. He stopped in the middle of his speech, looked out into the crowd, and said 'I would like to ask how many people here have relatives in the United States. Perhaps they could hold up their hands?' And a forest of hands arose on the spot, hands reaching out towards him, waving towards him, wanting to be seen by him. Whether you had a relative in the States or not, you put up your hand, for how else could you identify yourself to him? And he smiled, and said 'Well, I want to tell you they're doing well.'

He did it again in Galway, and it worked again. And he did it again in Limerick, before he left. 'I wonder before I go, if I could find out how many citizens here have relations in the United States. Do you think you could hold up your hands if you do?' Again the hands went up, again we claimed the honour of having scattered our families. And again we were awarded with a smile: 'No wonder there's so many of them over there.'

For decades those people in those crowds had listened to politicians and churchmen talking about the disgrace, the shame, the scandal of emigration. Yet here, on the streets of our cities, at the prompting of a showman's trick, we were holding up our hands to claim it, to wave it before the world. So desperate were we to respond to the first citizen of the great republic of the West that we could not be restrained from claiming our own disgrace. And in that, perhaps, for all the sham and neurosis of the event, there was some kind of healthy acknowledgement, some kind of truth. In the unseemly rush to claim Kennedy, we also had to claim all those other scattered families of ours, inglorious and unglamorous as they were. Those arms that reached out to him also had to grasp a painful history.

And, performer though he was, there is no reason to think that he was not also sincere in ways, that he was not also looking for something from us. Our hunger for his glamour, for his success, for his ease with the world and the flesh, was open, palpable, sometimes, as when the 'cream' of Irish society made a show of itself by mobbing him at a garden party in the grounds of Áras an Uachtarain, pathetic. But he too may have had both personal and political desires which only we could fulfil.

At a political level, the agenda of his speeches was so clear that only our euphoria could stop it from being heard. He harped continually on the war against communism, on the 'most difficult and dangerous struggle in the history of the world', and there was nothing secretive about his desire for Ireland to play its part in that struggle by joining NATO. Even the sentimental versions of Irish history which he repeated were carefully pointed in this direction: 'So Ireland is still old Ireland, but it has found a new mission in the 1960s, and that is to lead the free world, to join with other countries in the free world, to do in the 1960s what Ireland did in the early part of that century.'

But even in this there was an unmistakable sense of a man trying to convince himself, as well as his listeners, of something. By the time he came here, Kennedy had already committed over 12,000 American 'advisors' to Vietnam, and he felt, contemplating this anti-communist crusade, like an alcoholic contemplating the bottle. He had told Arthur Schlesinger what would happen in Vietnam: 'The troops will march in ... then we will be told we have to send in more troops. It's like taking a drink, the effect wears off and you have to have another.'

For a man slipping into disaster, and pulling his country with him, Ireland usefully blurred the issues. In Wexford town, he warned communist oppressors everywhere that they would 'do well to remember Ireland' and its long and ultimately successful fight against 'foreign domination'. In this rhetoric, he could, for a while, talk as the representative of a small oppressed nation rather than of a new imperial power asserting its control over Indochina. He could be Ho Chi Minh as well as John F. Kennedy, the plucky little guy standing up to the foreign bullies, as well as the imperial overlord sliding into a terrible war. No wonder he seemed to be enjoying himself.

This, too, may explain the odd clash of expectations which Kennedy's visit involved. He may have represented modernity and glamour and sophistication, but in fact his rhetoric about Ireland was of a sort that even de Valera could no longer get away with using. He talked about this 'green and misty isle', a phrase he had honed on the Irish-American circuit in the 1950s. He talked about loyalty to faith and fatherland. He talked about endurance and fortitude. He talked to us as if we were plucky little South Vietnam, a God-fearing peasant people who would always be loyal and always endure.

He didn't seem to know that what we wanted was to drive cars like his, to wear dark glasses like his, to be beautiful like him and Jackie, to be rich and happy, to shop in malls and bowl in alleys. He didn't seem to know that when he came the First Programme for Economic Expansion had just delivered increases of 20 per cent in purchasing power and wages. He didn't seem to know that in five years the rate of unemployment had dropped by 30 per cent and that in ten years the number of cars on the road had doubled. He didn't seem to know that while he was looking for a past, we were looking to him as an image of the future, that the confidence he would give us would be the confidence to outgrow our adoration of him.

There was a hint of this clash in Limerick when Francis Condell, the mayor, welcomed him by reminding him that 'we have seen the introduction to Ireland of a new type of American who is taking his place in our civic and social life, and who is bringing to our people the skills and techniques of industry', and asking please could we have some more of them in Limerick. In reply, Kennedy merely did his hands-up trick and quoted the words of 'Come back to Erin, mavourneen, mavourneen . . .' It was a silent movie and he was Valentino. We adored him, but there was no dialogue. If he had listened to the bells of Saint Nicholas Collegiate Church playing *The Star Spangled Banner* as he drove through Galway he might have understood better what faith and fatherland really meant to us.

In this confusion of desires, Kennedy created strange hybrid images of the Irish situation which mingled economic jargon and personal grief. He told us that 'most countries send out oil, iron, steel or gold, some others crops, but Ireland has only one export and that is people'. Later, he told us that 'other nations of the world, in whom Ireland has long invested her people, are now investing their capital as well as their vacations here in Ireland'.

In these images of Irish people as raw materials for export, as investments in foreign economies, of tourism as a fitting return for lost families, he spoke, without meaning to, a kind of truth that no Irish leader would have dared to utter. In those brutal words, intended to be soothing, he revealed the nature of the exchange in which Ireland was involved. In the middle of all the euphoria, all the self-delusion, he killed illusions about ourselves. When the euphoria was gone, and when the self-pity which followed his assassination in Dallas had dried up, those words remained as a clear description of our place in the world. By the time his image had faded in our heads and been obscured by sex stories and conspiracy theories, he had left us that accidental legacy of unpleasant but necessary truth. We faced the world thereafter with less innocence, less gullibility, more confidence and more clarity.

2.

'Ask not what your country can do for you,' said John F. Kennedy on the morning of his inauguration, 'ask what you can do for your country.' The ward bosses and the foot soldiers of the Irish-American political machine which had created the Kennedys as the first family probably wept into their beer at the stirring sentiments, but in their hearts of hairy bacon they knew better. Knowing precisely who did what for whom and what was given in return was the oil that made the machine work. Up in Chicago, Boss Daley may have had a flickering memory of the songs he sang on the campaign trail on the Irish South Side, getting out the vote for the man whose protégé he once was:

> *Whataya gonna do for McDonough?*
> *Whataya gonna do for YOU?*
> *Are ya gonna carry your precint?*
> *Are ya gonna be true blue?*
> *Whenever ya want a favour,*

The Lie of the Land

McDonough was ready to do.
Whataya gonna do for McDonough,
after what he has done for you?

As the Curse of the Kennedys rides again, returning like a battered mummy in a hammed-up Hammer Horror sequel, we glimpse again the spectre of tragedy that plays about Ireland's American dream. Between the idealism and the machinery lies a genuine sorrow about what the Irish can become and the debt we owe to history that stops us from becoming very much. In America and in Ireland we made political machines to defend ourselves with, to redress the balance of starvation and injustice and bigotry. We always believed we would do something with the machines that would be worthwhile, but we ended up trapped inside them, caught between what you can do for your country and what McDonough can do for you. The Kennedys are the ghosts in the Irish political machine. The tragedy is that the same machine that has delivered much of what is best in American politics in the last three decades can also turn its hand to digging up the dirt on a woman who says she was raped.

The great Irish contribution to politics is not any particular set of ideas but the political machine itself. It was born out of desperation and destitution, out of Daniel O'Connell and the Famine and No Irish Need Apply. The Irish must be one of the few peoples who had a highly sophisticated political system before they ever had a state. We had it in New York and Chicago and Boston, where the first Irish Boss, 'Mahatma' Lomasney, met the wretched immigrants on the wharfs and offered them a deal: 'Is somebody out of a job? We do our best to place him, and not necessarily on the public payroll. Does the family run in arrears with the butcher or the landlord? We lend a helping hand. Do the kids need clothing or the mother a doctor? We do what we can and, sure, as the world is run, such things must be done. We keep old friends and make new ones.'

In return, you voted the way you were told to vote. Lomasney developed the famous fine-tooth comb, with the teeth cut out in a pattern that, when superimposed on the ballot paper, showed exactly how to vote. And, sure, as the world was run who could blame the Irish, when they finally got their own state, for still seeing politics as a welfare state, for retaining a mental fine-tooth comb that could be applied to the ballot paper to give the right result?

Because the Irish were denied power for so long, power became its own end, a moral virtue in itself, a redressing of old wrongs even if it was not used to redress any new ones. When Honey Fitz Fitzgerald, father of Rose Kennedy, became the first mayor of Boston whose parents had been born in Ireland, thus founding the Kennedy dynasty of power, he shed a tear in his victory speech for his dead partners: 'It would have been a great delight to them for the natives of a country where democracy could not be exercised freely due to English domination.'

Being Irish meant that however rich and powerful you were, you carried with you the elan of the oppressed, just as, back home, being part of the national movement meant that you didn't have to actually tackle oppression: your very presence in power was a blow against oppression.

The problem for the Kennedys, like the problem for Irish politics at home, was that of bringing to life the ghost in the machine, the spirit of real political idealism that hovered somewhere around its cogs and wheels. Could you add intellectual substance and moral commitment to the machinations, or would such nebulous things be always chewed up in the innards of the machine? While the Kennedys were taking up the cause of Martin Luther King, the great Irish machine politician whom they needed for the purposes of power, Richard J. Daley, Boss of Chicago, was making speeches attacking 'pseudo-liberals, liberal intellectuals, suburban liberals, suburban liberal-intellectuals, and pseudo liberal-intellectual suburbanites'. But even this attack had little of conviction about it. When Daley was finally attacked himself at a Democratic party meeting by someone who pointed out that, without the liberals, the party would be nothing but a power-hungry skeleton, Daley brilliantly won the war before the conflict even got under way by simply declaring: 'I've always been a liberal myself.' It is a tactic that has been employed again in post-Robinsonian Ireland. The machine is neutral: to survive it will learn to love the goals it has previously despised. For it knows that there is really no goal but power.

Because of all this, the story of the Kennedys can never be merely what Peter Collier and David Horowitz call it in the subtitle to their book on the family, 'An American Drama'. It must also be, as they acknowledge in the first sentence of *The Kennedys*, 'an Irish tale' – a tale which goes back nearly 300 years to the day when a woman named Goody Glover was hanged as a witch on Boston Common because she'd knelt in front of the Blessed Virgin while telling her rosary beads in the 'devil's tongue' of Gaelic. The question which the Kennedy saga poses – whether the Irish political machine can ever drag itself away from its origins in the naked manipulation of power – is very much an Irish question, alive in the Ireland of 1991.

The Kennedys embody the Irish dream and the Irish nightmare. To go from the Mick Alleys and Paddyvilles of New York, Chicago and Boston to Palm Beach and Hyannisport, from Famine Irish to the White House before you can say (as Rose Kennedy was heard to say in the early days) 'When will the nice people of Boston accept us?' is the dream. To be dragged back down by the savage Mick that the nice people of Boston always knew was inside you, by the sex and drink and deathly urge to get one over on the other guy, is the nightmare.

In the dream, we get to the top on behalf of all the alienated and despised and discriminated-against races and nations. In the nightmare, we set our lawyers and detectives on the reputations of lower-class women who have dared to cross us. The dream still has enormous power in this country – if you are serving burgers in the Bronx, you are a potential Kennedy, if you are serving burgers in Castlebar, you are an actual nobody. We need the periodic re-emergence of the nightmare to remind us that the machine is not always a dream machine.

Maybe we need to wake up from the Kennedy dream before we can begin to get properly disillusioned with the machine and all its works. We still use the old Irish-American title for the head of the machine – Boss. And we still have the illusion that somehow or other a Kennedy can emerge from the machine, full of hope and idealism and generosity. Remembering that even the real Kennedys find it impossible to fully emerge, we should perhaps be a little more sceptical.

Or maybe, we will just accept the machine as it is and forget the dream altogether. Last year, a new restaurant opened in Dublin called after one of the legendary figures of Irish-American machine politics, Boss Croker. And just last weekend I wandered into another restaurant on Stephen's Green. On one wall was an enormous shrine with a huge portrait surrounded by the American colours. The portrait was of Mayor Richard J. Daley of Chicago, the Boss himself.

3.

Just after the Second World War, while the United Nations was being formed and the post-war world was taking shape, John F. Kennedy went to Hollywood with his friend Chuck Spalding, who worked as an assistant to Gary Cooper.

There were parties and starlets and drinking sessions. Much more important, though, there were ideas beginning to shape themselves in the future president's head. As he watched Gary Cooper and Clark Gable and Gene Tierney, Kennedy became fascinated 'by the way ordinary people came to inhabit the extraordinary celluloid identities created for them'.

As Spalding remembered it, 'Charisma wasn't a catchword

yet, but Jack was very interested in that blinding magnetism these screen personalities had. What exactly was it? How did you go about acquiring it? Did it have an impact on your private life? How did you make it work for you? He couldn't let the subject go.'

Due to the fascination which Ronald Reagan's background as a Hollywood actor engendered, it was easily forgotten that, however much Reagan represented an elision of real politics with screen fantasy, Kennedy had been there first and had achieved something much more profound. Reagan was a bad actor who became a bad president, but Kennedy was a man who set out to shape politics as a celluloid fiction.

His father had been a movie mogul, a creator of industrial fantasies, where Reagan had been a mere B-movie actor. Kennedy created first a literary then a cinematic image of himself. He won the presidency partly because he looked so much better on screen than Richard Nixon did. And, even before his death, he was played by an actor in a movie version of a real incident from his own life, *PT 109*.

Kennedy created an amalgam of fiction and reality in his own image which was so powerful that it has become stronger with the passage of time. In Dublin in March 1992 you could have read a big splash in the *Sunday Press* linking the deaths of Kennedy and of the screen idol Marilyn Monroe in a manner which, however dubious it might be as fact, seems unassailably appropriate as image. You could then have gone to *Conversations on a Homecoming* at the Abbey, a play haunted not by Kennedy but by the image of Kennedy as embodied in the tantalisingly absent figure J. J. Kilkelly, his small-town Irish imitator. And you could have gone to the Irish premiere of Oliver Stone's *JFK*, a film which takes the confusion of fiction and reality in the Kennedy image to yet further heights.

Kennedy's assassination, in itself, is the defining moment of the shift from the modern to the post-modern, from a relatively stable sense of the difference between art and life on the one hand, to the media culture which we now inhabit, in which we experience reality through electronic and celluloid media which constitute it as a work of art.

The reason we return to John Kennedy's death, and not to Robert's, is that John's is on television. When we run it through our heads, we run it in slow motion, in lurid newsreel colours. The bullet hitting his cavalcade is the inauguration of the media age, the first moment of history that is shared by everyone because it can be seen by everyone, over and over again.

It is significant that this sense of one cultural age passing and another being inaugurated was felt directly by artists. The playwright Arthur Miller puts it most succinctly in his autobiography *Timebends*: 'Even in the Thirties, as bad as things got, there was always the future; certainly in all my work was an implicit reliance on some redemptive time to come, a feeling that the cosmos cared about man, if only to mock him. With Kennedy's assassination, the cosmos had simply hung up the phone.'

To this death of an era there have been two kinds of artistic response. One, following on from Miller's sense of the loss of meaning, has been to see in Kennedy's death the image of a mocking kind of despair, the absurdity of catastrophe happening but the world going on as normal, failing to die when it so patently should. That is the feeling which runs through Tom Murphy's *Conversations on a Homecoming*. It is also the sense of Robert Patrick's play *Kennedy's Children*. Thomas Kinsella, in his poem for the tenth anniversary of Kennedy's death, *The Good Fight*, compares the world after the assassination to:

> . . . *a fish,*
> *flung back, that lay stunned,*
> *shuddered into consciousness,*
> *and dived back into the depths . . .*

That sense that what the world returned to after the shock of Kennedy's death was 'the depths' is, nevertheless, a reaction which makes sense only in the old world – the world where history is made up of events, and events are real, and real things change the world. There is, though, another kind of response, elicited both by the fact that Kennedy was an image as much as he was a real person and by the power of his death as a media image rather than as history.

This response relates to a different, post-modern world, one where history is made up of images and images are infinitely recyclable and nothing ever changes.

The great American artist Robert Rauschenberg already used photographs of Kennedy in his 1960s 'combine paintings', along with eagles, ropes and bits of rag. Kennedy was an object which could be made into a work of art, a part of the melding of art and reality that was central to Rauschenberg's strategy: 'My works have the value of reality ... my combine paintings are actual.'

As, in post-modern culture, history comes to be regarded as a storehouse of images rather than a record of events, the historical event of Kennedy's assassination is converted into *The Book of Genesis* of the media world, the great point at which real events became free-floating images, there to be used and re-used regardless of any historical meaning.

This sense of Kennedy's death as above all a photograph or technological image of reality itself reaches its zenith in Don DeLillo's superb novel *Libra*, which blends invention and reality with breathtaking skill.

Here is DeLillo's description of the assassination: 'A woman with a camera turned and saw that she was being photographed. A woman in a dark coat was aiming a Polaroid right at her. It was only then she realised she'd just seen someone shot in her own viewfinder.' Jack Ruby watches the killing over and over again on television: 'It was almost as though they were re-enacting the crucifixion of Jesus.'

That sense of re-enactment dovetails with Arthur Miller's

more conventional, if more despairing, reaction – the feeling that there was now no future, and that our sense of time and history is out of joint. Where there is no future tense, the past tense and the present tense don't quite work either.

The endless, numbing return to the moment of Kennedy's assassination, the obsessive search for theories that will fill the black holes of that static darkness, is the mark of a culture that has nowhere to go but round in circles.

4.

There is a strange optimism about conspiracy theories. In spite of the dark mutterings, the invisible hands, the malign forces that control our destinies, the world of the conspiracy is a paradoxically comforting one. The conspiracy is the God of a Godless world. God may not be in his heaven, but someone after all is up there controlling things, making things happen, giving a shape to an otherwise terrifyingly random world.

Believing that the awful violence and chaos of the world you live in is merely what it appears to be is a sickening kind of disillusion. Being able to trace in those events the work of an evil mind or minds relieves that pain. There is, as we know in Ireland, a strong connection between the religious mind and the conspiratorial psyche: God and the conspiracy stem from the same need to see an order amidst chaos.

It is this connection which gives Oliver Stone's remarkable *JFK* its ecstatic, almost religious quality. In that painful ecstasy, fact and fiction, history and invention, are distinctions which cease to matter.

JFK is paradoxical in other, more direct matters of form and content. On the one hand there is the *JFK* which is probably the most profound incursion of the technologies and attitudes of pop video, even of experimental 'art' video, into the mainstream cinema. There is the almost literally stunning sensory overload, the speed of the camera and the editing deceiving not merely the eye but the brain.

We move between not two but three layers of reality – actual documentary footage, fiction film and, most disturbing, re-invented documentary film: scenes we are familiar with from television news footage, but which have been re-staged with a disorientating mixture of period accuracy and anachronistic technological representation.

While this is happening to your eyes something analogous is being done to your ears, pounded as they are by a soundtrack in which 'natural' sounds like the revving of engines or the scything of plants melt indistinguishably into the pounding of drums or the rattle of maracas. Even the more conventional musical aspects of the score create this same sense of the confusion of opposites, with the stately tones of the great Irish lament *Marbhna Luimni* inextricably interwoven with Latin American percussion.

In the midst of this barrage of the senses, you sit awed and numbed like a devotee at a religious ritual, entranced and mesmerised as the screen circles back and back again to the sacred moment of the assassination.

Yet interwoven with this strange avant-garde film of disloca-tion and disorientation is another movie, one which is conven-tional to the point of sentimentality and nostalgia. Where the first movie is stunningly futuristic in its form, this second one is incredibly nostalgic in its content. It is Frank Capra revisited, a remake of *Mr Smith Goes to Washington* (1939).

Kevin Costner's Jim Garrison is Jimmy Stewart as the small-town lawyer taking on the Washington establishment. Costner, indeed, plays not so much Garrison as Stewart. There is the same slow drawl, the same innocent perplexity at the evils of the world, the same appeal to good old-fashioned middle-American patriotism. The supreme irony of *JFK* is that it is this good old-fashioned American movie, and not the weird technological post-modern movie that is interwoven with it, that causes the profound political unease about the confusion of history and intention which the film induces.

For me at least, the intercuttings and the editings, the obsessive returns to and reinventions of the assassination itself, are the parts of *JFK* which ring most true. This is so, not in spite of the fact that they play dazzling games with the idea of what is real, but because of it. There is a genuine sort of truth in the sense of disorientation which they induce, and in their location of the beginning of that sense of disorientation in the moment of assassination. The assassination does mark the inauguration of a post-modern world of confusion between media and reality, and I know of no better evocation of that aspect of our world than *JFK*.

This radical and stunning evocation of what it is like to live in the western world now, is, unfortunately, not enough for Oliver Stone. He also wants to evoke the feeling of a prelapsarian American Utopia before the fall of the assassination. The side of *JFK* which is seeking to recreate the world of Frank Capra – decent, God-fearing, good-living men who stood up for truth in a society that, however corrupt, would ultimately be unable to resist their idealism – is, ironically, the one which is most economical with the truth. In making *Mr Garrison Goes To Washington*, Stone has to conform to the demands of the genre. And the main demand of the genre is that Jimmy Stewart has to be not merely good but right. Jim Garrison has to be right.

Stone had available to him a story that would have avoided the pitfalls he stumbles into. Garrison could still have been the centre of the movie, could still, even, have been an archetypally good man. The story of a good man trying to locate himself within a world where reality has become unattainable, a man becoming ever more obsessive and even further from discovering the key to what he is trying to discover, would have matched Stone's methods.

At times, Stone seems close to making this movie. But the essential conservatism of his vision, requiring as it does the symbol of an older purer America, imposes the need for a Garrison who is not a good man descending into madness in his pursuit of a truth, but a man who is right in all things, whose theories have to be endorsed. Thus even though the evidence of the film itself suggests that Garrison's prosecution of Clay Shaw is a show trial and an abuse of justice, it has to be presented as a great moral crusade.

This conservatism has its nasty side, too. Stone's vision of a good, decent America is articulated in the film through a dangerously simplistic set of contrasting images. The good guys are handsome, normal-looking and rooted in the nuclear family. The bad guys are peculiar-looking, physically imperfect and homosexual.

And Stone uses these contrasts with a chilling brilliance in which physical and sexual normality become moral categories rather than merely descriptive facts. In his rage at what America has become, Stone draws on both the benign decency of an older America and its dangerous and claustrophobic simplicities.

Hung as it is between a nostalgic past tense and a futuristic vision of society, between *Mr Smith Goes to Washington* and *1984, JFK* is a powerful document of a time which feels itself to have only a past tense and a future tense, but no present tense, no stable point in the present from which to define itself.

The film's tragedy, though, is that it ends up being not a critique of this condition, but a stunning example of it.

1994

Mixed Blessings

The End of the Irish Church

In English, the days of the week take their names from a curiously promiscuous collection of gods, Roman, Viking, and Pagan, from Saturn to Woden to the Moon. In Irish, three days are named after, not Gods, but penitential religious practices. The Irish for Wednesday translates as 'first fast', for Friday as 'the fast', and for Thursday as 'the day between the two fasts'. Wednesday and Friday were, in the great Irish monasteries, days of fasting and mortification. Thus, in Ireland, the everyday has been literally defined, not by wandering gods, but by religious practice. For much of Irish history, the sacred and the secular have been virtually indistinguishable.

Catholicism in Ireland has long been a nationality as much as a religion. The words 'Irish Catholic' do not denote merely a person of a specific faith born in a specific country. They have also come to stand for some third thing born out of the fusion of the other two – a country, a culture, a politics. Catholicism in Ireland has been a matter of public identity more than of private faith, and the struggle to disentangle the two is what defines the Irish Church now.

In Ireland, as in some other atypical European countries, such as Poland and Croatia, where political nationality was often tenuous or submerged, the Church became a kind of surrogate State, the only organised and institutionalised expression of nationality. Modern Ireland, in its attempt to become a European republican democracy, has had to struggle with the fact that the Church was there before the State, that it can claim, and often has claimed, prior rights over the territory. The State is young and fragile, with only 70 years behind it. The Church is old and seasoned, so old that its language and culture, its imagery and its power, have seeped into the society.

It is not just a matter of a strongly religious culture, though it remains true that Ireland is exceptionally religious by the standards of the western world. More people attend church once a week in Ireland (86 per cent of the overwhelmingly Catholic population) than in any other Judaeo-Christian society in the world. Asked how important God is in their lives, the Irish come out far ahead of any nation in Europe. When it comes to belief in the existence of the soul, in life after death, in heaven, in prayer, the Irish score so much higher in surveys than the rest of the developed world as to seem not part of that world at all. Yet even this is not what is at issue, for such things remain, however deeply held, still matters of private belief.

It is the public nature of Catholicism in Ireland that has really marked it off. The founding act of the modern Irish State – the 1916 Rising – is a religious as much as a political act, and conceived by its leader, Patrick Pearse, as such. Its symbolic occurrence at Easter, its conscious imagery of blood sacrifice and redemption, shaped a specifically Catholic political con-sciousness that belied the secular republican aims of many of the revolutionaries. Irish nationalism, the primary driving force of Irish politics for most of this century, became, in both its constitutional and its violent manifestations, intimately entwined with Catholicism. Eamon de Valera saw fit to get John Charles McQuaid, the Catholic Archbishop of Dublin, to help him to write the Constitution. In the early 1980s, IRA prisoners in Northern Ireland staged a hunger strike whose imagery and effect were inextricable from the penitential and martyrological traditions of Irish Catholicism.

In less directly political ways, too, the Church had an enormous public presence. The sociologist Tom Inglis has pointed out that in Ireland it was the Catholic Church which, in the nineteenth century, taught the peasant Irish not merely what to believe but how to behave. It was the Church which took an agricultural people used to landscape and the rhythms of the farming day, and taught them how to inhabit public spaces and respect modern, industrialised time-keeping. Forms of behaviour and control were inculcated by the Church in a manner which went far beyond the spiritual and into the realms of secular time and space.

And if the Church 'civilised' the Wild Irish, it also provided the trappings of a State where there was no State. The Church successfully outmanoeuvred the British government's attempts to construct a secular education system, and built its own mass education system under the control of religious brothers and nuns. It founded its own universities and hospitals. An Irish person was, and is, likely to be born in a Catholic hospital, educated at Catholic schools, married in a Catholic church, have children named by a priest, be counselled by Catholic marriage advisors if the marriage runs into trouble, be dried out in Catholic clinics for the treatment of alcoholism if he or she develops a drink problem, be operated on in Catholic hospitals, and be buried by Catholic rites. The 'cradle to grave' attention of European social welfare systems was created in Ireland by the Church.

Having built all of these institutions as alternatives to British rule, the Church retained them in an Independent Ireland, and remains a massive temporal power, controlling most of the health and education systems and having a large influence in all other social services. Most primary schools are in Church ownership, as are 90 per cent of secondary schools. Teacher training is Church controlled, as are most of the training hospitals in which nurses and doctors are formed. In a real and immediate sense, the Church has successfully interposed itself between the personal worlds of education (mind) and illness (body) on the one hand, and the impersonal world of State services and institutions on the other. Holding that ground has given it enormous temporal, as well as spiritual, power.

Yet this great monolith is not all that it seems. The Irish Catholic Church is also a troubled institution, suffering a serious loss of authority. Its very strengths throughout the centuries have also become weaknesses in the Ireland of the 1990s. It is afflicted with a paradoxical problem: it cannot hope to retain power without giving up power. Two of its greatest bulwarks have become barriers.

The first strength that is now becoming a weakness lies in the very nature of Irish Catholicism itself. It achieved and retained its power through the centuries not by being simply the rock of Peter, but by being something much more like a geological section in which layer after layer of rock is submerged beneath the surface. It grew and consolidated itself not by obliterating what was there before, but by adding another layer to its surface.

Early Irish Christianity, for instance, flourished not by wiping out the earlier Celtic beliefs, but by adapting them. To this day, the annual pilgrimage on the last Sunday in July up Croagh Patrick mountain in Mayo re-enacts the worship of the mountain gods in a Catholic context. Early Irish Christian spirituality is marked by both the intimacy of a tribal society and by a use of natural imagery bordering on pantheism. John Scotus Eriugena (the name meaning John the Irishman, born in Eire), the greatest philosopher and theologian of the early Middle Ages, was indeed accused of pantheism, his great book *De Divisione Naturae* burned by order of the Council of Paris in 1210, and placed on the Vatican index in 1685.

These stresses on the 'Irish' part of 'Irish Catholicism' are best summed up in the famous Irish mediaeval monastic poem:

> *Who to Rome goes*
> *Much labour, little profit knows.*

Mixed Blessings

For God, on earth though long you've sought him,
You'll miss at Rome unless you've brought him.

This tendency to localism and independence, to build on what is in Ireland rather than on a simple universalism, helped Irish Catholicism to survive persecution and isolation under centuries of British rule. But it also forged a kind of Catholicism that is highly dependent on the nature of Irish society. So long as the society remained relatively stable, this rootedness was a huge strength. But, in a shifting society, the Church's very close relationship to the place and the people means that the Church feels the pressure of change even more intimately than would otherwise be the case.

At a popular level, and often to the discomfort of the Catholic hierarchy, the early kind of pagan Catholicism remains very much alive. In many rural areas, acts of devotion at, for instance, Holy Wells, vestigial shrines of forgotten water spirits, survive in a christianised form. From time to time, too, there are outbreaks of superstitious enthusiasm, such as the craze for 'moving' statues of the Blessed Virgin which swept much of the country in 1985 and 1986. In some places, such as Knock, in County Mayo, visited by Pope John Paul II in 1979, this religion of magic has been fully institutionalised by the Church. But in others, it remains on the fringe of Catholicism, barely accommodated by a church all too aware of its capacity to take on a life of its own.

The modern Irish Church, however, was built in the nineteenth century by the imposition on this native layer of religion of a particularly harsh and autocratic combination of sexual puritanism and centralised bureaucracy. Both owed their success to the trauma of Famine, the catastrophe of the mid nineteenth century which halved the population in a few decades. Because the Famine had been caused at least in part by over-population, the new combination of French Jansenism and English Puritanism which the Church adopted made a kind of bitter economic sense and eventually led to a situation in the 1950s where Ireland had the lowest marriage rate in the world.

At the same time, the institutionalisation of the Church as an obedient, highly organised, highly efficient bureaucracy, also had economic roots in the Church's position after the Famine as one of the few sources of wealth and development and social services that the Catholic Irish had. On the one hand, the jobs of priest and nun provided an acceptable economic status for surplus children. On the other, the massive church and school building programmes undertaken in the latter half of the nineteenth century were Ireland's form of infrastructural development.

A religion that had been local, intimate and more spiritual than devotional, became a massively effective power structure. Between 1850 and 1900, Mass attendance rose from an estimated 30–40 per cent to the 90 cent cent level which it retained up to the 1980s. But, as the Redemptorist priest Fr John J. O'Riordain has put it, 'The whole progress of the nineteenth century in Ireland, with its renewal of church structures, training of clergy, building of churches, expansion of religious life, and devotional revolution, might well be seen as one triumphal march. But the truth, to my mind, is less flattering. Success there was beyond doubt. But the progress was not so much earned as gained in a somewhat dishonest manner. At best it was a display of wealth by somebody who had received a legacy.'

That legacy, though, lasted well into the 1980s. The groundwork laid down in the nineteenth century was the basis for the Church's triumph in independent Ireland. Once there was an Irish state, it became the effective arbiter of social legislation, having a ban on divorce inserted into the Constitution, encouraging the introduction of draconian censorship of books and films, delaying the legalisation of artificial contraception until 1979, retaining largely unquestioned control over schools and hospitals funded by the taxpayer, resisting the slow development of a welfare state.

Yet this very success also carried the seeds of failure. Simply because its triumph was so complete, the Irish Catholic Church did not have to develop the kind of complex lay culture which the Catholic Church built in other European Catholic countries like France and Spain and Italy.

Because the media were mostly very respectful of the Church, there was no need for specifically Catholic newspapers or broadcasting stations. Because the trade unions were only marginally 'infested' by Marxism or secular radicalism, there was no need for specifically Catholic trade unions. Because all of the functioning political parties were fundamentally Catholic, there was no need for a specifically Catholic political party. Thus Ireland, the most unequivocally Catholic society in Europe, has none of these things to this day.

Essentially, the Catholic Church exercised its power at the top and at the bottom, but not in the middle of the social process. At the top, there were secret meetings with government ministers and political leaders at which the Church could exercise great influence. At the bottom, there was the long-term power of controlling education and shaping minds. But in the middle, there was no genuinely Catholic intelligentsia and no Catholic civil society.

In the last decade, the top and bottom layers of influence have run into deep trouble. At the top, the Church's political influence has become steadily more marginal. The Church scored two great political victories in the 1980s, by using its influence in favour of a constitutional amendment to ban abortion and against a constitutional amendment to permit divorce. In both cases, it was on the winning side, and succeeded in holding the line against the march of secular liberalism. In both cases, however, the victories were pyrrhic, achieved at the cost of a break in the politico-moral consensus that ultimately undermined the Church's authority as being 'above politics'. By 1990, it was possible for the leader of one of Ireland's major political parties, aligned to the Christian

Democrats in Europe, to refer to an unnamed bishop in public as a 'bastard'.

In the case of divorce, it is now accepted as inevitable that Ireland will introduce divorce laws in the 1990s, and even the most stalwart supporter of the Church line, Fianna Fáil, has proposed to do so.* In the case of abortion, the 1983 'pro-life' amendment to the Constitution recognising the right to life of the unborn foetus not only made abortion a matter of public controversy and thus increased public support for it in certain circumstances, it also led to the legalisation of abortion itself. In 1992, the Supreme Court, faced with the case of a fourteen-year-old girl who had been raped and was pregnant and suicidal, decided that under the 'pro-life' clause itself, she had the right to an abortion in Ireland.

In the subsequent referendum to roll back this judgement, the Church, for the first time in living memory, was clearly divided and marginalised, with the bishops collectively telling the faithful that they could vote either way, but individual bishops, including the powerful Archbishop of Dublin, Desmond Connell, taking a much harder line. The magisterial authority of the Church has been fatally undermined.

For different reasons, the bottom layer of influence has also become much more tenuous. Keeping control of schools and hospitals and other public services is a highly effective way of maintaining power, but it is also highly labour-intensive. It requires the kind of mass recruitment of clergy and nuns which made it possible up until the early 1970s for most Irish families to boast a member in holy orders. Such recruitment fell away almost completely during the 1970s, and has not recovered since. The shock troops of Church control in education, the Christian Brothers, are moribund, with barely enough recruits to look after the aged Brothers in retirement, never mind control

* Divorce laws were in fact introduced in 1996.

and teach in hundreds of schools. Likewise most orders of nuns and priests. In the 1990s, the Church has been forced to retreat ever further into management of schools and hospitals, leaving the groundwork to lay personnel who are increasingly difficult to control.

At the same time, there are signs of increasing radicalism amongst those who do join or stay in religious orders. The extraordinary missionary tradition which sent thousands of Irish priests and nuns to a 'spiritual empire' in Africa, Asia and Latin America has, in a sense, reversed itself, with returned missionaries importing the ideas of liberation theology and the option for the poor, ideas which threaten rather than reinforce, the Church's place within Irish power structures.

In the 1990s, much of the most radical campaigning on issues of poverty and exclusion in Ireland has come from the Conference of Major Religious Superiors, representative of the large orders of priests and nuns. When the former Taoiseach, Charles Haughey, remarked in reply to an attack from the CMRS on his economic policies that he did not trust organisations with words like 'major' and 'superior' in their titles, it was a mark both of the perceived incongruity of this political radicalism on the part of the Church, and of the difficulty which the political establishment often has with it.

Perhaps even more profoundly threatening to the institutional power of the Church is the quiet spread of feminism within its ranks. Nuns, for so long the obedient servants of the magisterium, have begun to threaten its authority, causing the eminent Catholic sociologist Father Liam Ryan to remark that the Church treats women like second-class citizens but must remember that 'male geriatric dictatorship may well have been what finally topped Communism in Eastern Europe'.

Recognising that its power was threatened at the top and at the bottom in these ways, the Irish Church began to slowly accommodate itself to what was in the middle, the new Irish civil society which emerged from urbanisation and industrialisation in the 1960s. Early in that decade John Charles McQuaid, returning from the Second Vatican Council, told his Irish flock, 'Allow me to reassure you, no change will worry the tranquillity of your Christian lives.' By the early seventies, the Church was trying to jettison that grand paternalism and present instead the image of bishops who could sing on chat shows.

It had, however, underestimated the omnivorous power of the new media. By 1992, the bishop who was best at singing on chat shows, Bishop Eamonn Casey of Galway, appointed as the friendly face who could win through media charm the authority which the Church had previously maintained by haughty power, himself became a victim of the ultimate resistance to authority of the modern media. The *Irish Times* uncovered the fact that Bishop Casey had used diocesan funds for payments to the mother of his secret son in America. A sex scandal at the height of the Irish Catholic Church, the last unthinkable event, had happened, and the Church discovered that it could not be at one and the same time magisterial and populist, that if you tried to show a friendly face you could not control what would in fact be revealed.

This final loss of authority has probably placed the Irish Church on an inexorable path of institutional change. It also explains why the Church cannot retain power without giving up power.

At the level of institutional, bureaucratic and political power that it attained for itself in the nineteenth century, the Irish Church is mortally wounded. Its institutions are increasingly challenged from within, and its political power, though still considerable, is rapidly on the wane. The demands of a young, highly educated population and the needs of a pluralist society to disentangle itself from the tribal religions that have made violence endemic in Northern Ireland both mean that the Church's grip on political power will continue to weaken.

But it is important to remember that it is really only this nineteenth-century Church that is in sharp decline. The Church on which it imposed itself, the intimate, pantheistic and spiritual Church which had shown itself to be virtually invulnerable to persecution and poverty, even if Mass attendance was relatively low, shows no sign of rapid decline. What Father Liam Ryan describes as 'the four deadly sins of Irish Catholicism' – 'an obsession with sexual morality, clerical authoritarianism, anti-intellectualism, or at best non-intellectualism, and the creation of a ghetto mentality' – will, ironically, become less important as the faithful vote with their feet and choose simply to ignore Church teaching on sexuality, do the same with clerical authority, develop their own intellects, and step out of their ghettos. In a sense, the more easily Irish Catholics reject the Church for its sins, the more easily will the religious culture which, like it or not, they have inherited, sit with them. The chances are that the Irish Church in the year 2000 will look remarkably like what it was in 1800 – a focus for a relaxed but deep spirituality in which the broad culture rather than the devotional and behavioural rules is what matters.

1995

Annie and the Bishop,
Ireland and America

In May 1992 it was revealed that the Bishop of Galway, Eamonn Casey, had fathered a child. His lover, Annie Murphy, then published a book giving explicit details of their affair.

Just before you turn off the main road towards Mullaghmore Interpretative Centre, now one of the most symbolic sites in Ireland, there is a ruined old church in Kilnaboy that is, in its way, yet more powerfully symbolic. Roofless and open to the elements, it has yet survived the centuries and its grey, hand-cut stones embody the unadorned endurance of the Irish Catholic Church, its gravity and its ascetic beauty. Just over the doorway, though, is a sheela-na-gig, a grotesquely sexual and sternly obscene figure of a woman exposing herself. The same monks who prayed and fasted here placed this figure of terrifying womanhood at the centre of their church, a reminder, perhaps, of the flesh they had to fear and shun.

Annie Murphy is the Irish Catholic Church's sheela-na-gig made flesh, an avenging spirit risen up from the dark of the celibate mind to haunt and to terrify, to embody all those dangerous thoughts subdued by prayer and fasting. She is their worst nightmare come true, a figure from the mediaeval witch-hunters' manuals: wild and indiscreet, loose-tongued and lusty. She has written a book about her love affair with a bishop, a book that is full not just of sex, but of the body itself, of beard rash and high blood pressure, of colitis and groin infections, of cancers and amputations. Of all the ills and sins that flesh is heir to.

In Irish folklore, the priest's mistress is a figure of almost supernatural evil. One old Gaelic proverb tells of 'three who will never see the light of Paradise':

> *The angel of pride,*
> *The unbaptised child,*
> *And a priest's concubine.*

The angel of pride is Satan. The priest's concubine (ceile shagairt) is associated with him. So, too, is the buried child, the forgotten child, the child interred at night in unconsecrated ground. For some true believers, no doubt, Annie Murphy and her son, her long-buried child, will still be associated with the satanic. Her book will be not just an act of personal betrayal, but an act of sacrilege.

Both of these roles – sheela-na-gig to terrify the Irish Church, and desecrator of the faithful's ideas of the sacred – are ones which Annie Murphy is happy to play in her book. They are, after all, starring roles, big parts in a drama that has been played for centuries. To describe making love in the bishop's palace in Killarney, to describe distracting the bishop while he is saying Mass, to mention his cross and ring in the context of furtive coupling, is to be one of the two main players, not in the kitchen tragedy of Annie and Eamonn, but in the grand opera of the clash of eternal forces. It is to play Body to his Soul, avenging angel to his tarnished saint, world, flesh and devil to his Father, Son and Holy Ghost. It is a lot more glorious than to be poor, wounded Annie.

Yet the real story, the story that comes through so painfully in her book once you get used to the strange circumstances of this love affair, is ineffably ordinary. Take away the one sensational aspect of the story – that the man involved is a Catholic bishop, sworn to celibacy and preaching a strict code of sexual morality – and what you are left with is a story that life has told over and over, until it is blue in the face.

A younger, more vulnerable woman meets an older, more powerful man. He dazzles her with his power, his confidence, his command of the world. They fall in love and begin a sexual relationship. He promises her nothing but he doesn't need to for, hurt and abused as she is, she is more than capable of making him into a promise to herself. She gives him pleasure, excitement and adoration. He gives her the first two but probably not the third. She thinks of the future, he thinks of the present, floating on the delusion that he can have the best of all worlds. He makes her pregnant. The baby forces choices on her, choices which, because he is a man and a powerful one, he doesn't believe he has to make. He behaves badly, hypocritically, politically. It ends in tears: first hers, then, after many years, his.

Take away the thrill of discovering that bishops as a class are no better than many other men, and what remains is the fact that they are no worse. Little would have to change in Annie Murphy's book if Eamonn Casey were a prominent politician, or a judge, or just an ordinary married man indulging in a passionate but doomed side-affair which he will shake off when it becomes too threatening to his marriage and his settled place in the world. Desecration lies in the treacherous, abusive things that people do to each other, not in the fact that they are done in a bishop's palace rather than a bedsit.

We were promised some shocking revelations: that the affair lasted longer than was previously believed and continued after the birth of their son, Peter; that it was conducted for a period in a car parked in a gravel pit in Dublin; that they slept together again in a New York hotel as recently as early 1991. But given the initial premise – that an Irish bishop had an affair and a child – and the inevitable deceptions and moral contortions that flow from it, these are not shocking at all. They come with the territory, and the territory is a well-worn ground of deceit and double-dealing, a landscape that is there whether bishops choose to tread on it or not.

Annie and the Bishop, Ireland and America

What is actually much more striking in Annie Murphy's story is the shock of the familiar. The view from the bishop's bed is a new angle on the sumptuousness and luxury of life at the top of the clerical ladder. There is nothing shocking in the notion that some bishops live in palaces, eat like kings and behave like princelings, that they are often waited on, flattered and pampered. But this is seldom described, because outsiders do not get close enough to do so. Annie Murphy is one outsider who did, who became privy to a world whose sensual delights may exclude sex but include the best food and drink, the finest places to live, the swankiest cars, clothes bought straight from Harrods. She is a privileged reporter, and the value of her testimony lies at least as much in its description of things that are taken for granted by the faithful, as of things that will shock and horrify them.

If there is an extraordinary dimension to this story of ordinary things, it is not the clash of sacred and secular, but the clash of Ireland and Irish-America. Annie Murphy's family could have been invented by Eugene O'Neill, such is its archetypal drama of lace curtain Irish respectability riddled with alcoholism, subdued violence and the hard bitterness of exile. John Steinbeck looked at the Irish-Americans and said that they 'do have a despairing gaiety, but they also have a dour and brooding ghost that rides on their shoulders and peers in on their thoughts'. Annie Murphy embodies both the despairing gaiety and the brooding ghost, with a view of the world that is often wildly comic and often haunted by nameless forebodings.

Her love for Eamonn Casey seems inextricable from her love for Ireland, an exile's love of the dream homeland. She is in love with the place as much as with the man. The sea, the mountains, the flowers are characters in her love affair. She brings to that affair both the illusory longing and the driven ambition of Irish-America, both the rosy view of Ireland and the all-American drive to make the world conform to her view of it.

In many ways Eamonn Casey is as typically Irish as she is

Irish-American. Energetic, garrulous, at home with the world, but also full of evasions and denials. In certain ways she is more ambitious than he is, for she wants the world to change, wants a clerical princeling to come down off his throne and take charge of her messy life, while he wants things to be the same only more so. He wants everything he has and something else as well – the joy of sex, maybe the comfort of being loved rather than adored. He just has to make room in his busy life for another pleasure. She has to re-invent the world, make it conform to her desires. It is a clash of mother country and restless exile as much as it is a clash of Mother Church and restless desire.

As in a Greek play, the clash of these incompatible but ineluctable forces can produce only tragedy. The directness which the Irish learned in America cannot communicate with the evasions of life at home. The elaborate cathedral of airy self-justifications which he builds on the restless foundations of his desire is demolished by her impatience. The ambition of her desire, the vision of a future in which she and Eamonn and Peter will live happily ever after, is thwarted by his ability to live with all his contradictions in a never-ending present rather than have to face the hard choices for the future.

The tragedy, strangely, is at its sharpest when the story is most comic. The awful events – the abandonment of a son and the humiliation of an important public man – are awful only because there is a glimmer that things might have been other-wise. What is most wretched about the abandonment of Peter is that there are times when there is another sort of abandonment, times when Annie and Eamonn seem to have abandoned themselves to a kind of exuberant madness in which their laughter mingled into one wild cascade.

There are episodes in their story during which the absurdity of their situation is funny instead of sordid, during which they seem to have been able to stand back and look at themselves and collapse in a helpless laughter.

That kind of removal from oneself, that release into a zone

where nothing matters, is what lovers call love and saints call a state of grace. Though the faithful may think it blasphemous, it is nevertheless possible that in those moments of wild laughter Eamonn Casey and Annie Murphy were in love and in a state of grace at the same time.

If that is so, then it is also possible that the real sacrilege in relation to Annie Murphy's story would be not to allow for those moments when the sacred and the secular, the soul and the body, the monk and the sheela-na-gig, sex and holiness, were, however fleetingly, one and the same thing. Because the story is so public, so symbolic, it is easy to overlook this precious intimacy at its core, the sacred humanity without which there would be no tragedy.

Tragedies are supposed to teach us something, and what is to be learned from the tragedy of these hurt people is that a world which insists on neat divisions between the holy and the unholy, between men and women, between courage and hypocrisy, is one which creates tragedies.

Brecht replied to the adage 'unhappy the land that has no heroes' with the correction 'unhappy the land that needs heroes'. Equally, unhappy the Church that needs heroes, that is so threatened and terrified by the revelation that within its upper ranks there exist ordinary human desires and ordinary human hypocrisies. All Annie Murphy has really done is to state the obvious. That she can gain so much notice from doing so is the fault of those who have denied the obvious for too long.

William Butler Yeats stated the obvious more elegantly many years ago in a poem called *Crazy Jane Talks With The Bishop*:

> *A woman can be proud and stiff*
> *When on love intent;*
> *But Love has pitched his mansion in*
> *The place of excrement;*
> *For nothing can be sole or whole*
> *That has not been rent.*

Whether the bishop listened to Crazy Jane or not, Yeats does not tell us. It would be nice to think, though, that some bishops might listen to the strange, abandoned laughter of Annie Murphy and Eamonn Casey before they became hateful and afraid.

1993

Dev's People

The nun, Mrs Gorman remembers, knew what she wanted. Mrs Gorman keeps the keys to de Valera's Cottage, the neat little house at Knockmore, just outside Bruree, that is now a shrine to the memory of the patriarch. The roses that used to grow outside the door have been taken up and replaced with traditional paving stones. The cooker has been taken out from the grate and replaced with a traditional open hearth, the old iron kettle hanging from its hook. The lino has been taken from the floor and replaced with traditional flagstones. The bareness of the walls is broken by a holy trinity: a statue of the Blessed Virgin, a print of Daniel O'Connell and an embroidered American eagle in a frame.

The nun, though, was not much interested in these downstairs room. She climbed the steep, narrow stairs that led to what was once Eamon de Valera's bedroom. The bed, Mrs Gorman warned her, might be a bit dusty. She didn't mind. She climbed up on de Valera's old iron bed and lay there, her black habit spread out against the pink mattress. She looked up at the whitewashed sloping sides of the ceiling or, perhaps, out the tiny square window at the small patch of ground where, in his boyhood, as he later told the Dail, young Eamon learned everything from 'the spancelling of a goat to the milking of a cow'. After a few minutes she got out of the bed, came down the stairs looking contented and left.

Up the road, in another of the neat villages that dot this gentle Limerick pastureland, there is a woman in her late thirties. 'I'm married,' she says, 'but we've been separated for eight years. He went off his own way and I've looked after our two daughters. One of them's still in school, but the other's in

London. I have a man who comes in to me a few times a week, but he's afraid to move in with me. Not that the priests bother you any more. I had one nasty experience a while back, when a mother and daughter, who I can tell you were doing all they wanted to do themselves but liked to complain about other people, put the priest on to me. But that didn't last long – there's so much going on around here now that they just don't bother any more. Still, as soon as my youngest one is reared, I'm getting out.'

The young man who works in the garage in Bruree and is going home to Kilmallock and then, maybe, out to Madonna's Nite Club in Charleville, knows all about leaving. 'There used to be ten of us would go out together every Saturday night. After this week, I'm the only one left. There's a whole street in Elephant and Castle, it's more Kilmallock than Kilmallock, if you know what I mean. Sure, there's all that history around here, but what difference does it make? The young people just aren't interested in politics.'

Yet the past has its power around here, not least because the present keeps returning to it. At Knocklong, the railway station has closed and the bus just comes once a day. The maple-floored ballroom is closed up and the hotel no longer takes guests. There used to be traditional music a few years ago, played by an Australian couple and an Irishman, but the Australians went home. The Bord Fáilte traditional holiday cottages have been sold off. The days of turmoil when Bruree and Knocklong knew not one civil war but two – the big one when two thousand Republicans fought two thousand Free Staters for control of the Kilmallock Triangle, and the little one a year before when workers in both villages declared themselves Soviets and flew the red flag for a few days – are long gone.

What remains of those days is the de Valera Museum in the old schoolhouse in Bruree. Here you can see the relics of a famous man's life: a headline copy book with the curling, punctilious handwriting – 'Queen Victoria was born 24 May 1819'. A jacket with a Fainne worked in thread on the label. Prizes won at sports meetings and War of Independence medals. Rosary beads, prayer books, spectacles, a walking stick. The old school desk with the carved initials 'ED' that had to be deepened and enhanced before the museum was opened in 1972. And, more than these things, the words that de Valera spoke at an after-Mass meeting in Bruree in 1955 and that still remain in the hearts of many who live in and around the village: 'The Irish language is the bond that keeps our people together throughout the centuries, and enabled them to resist all the efforts to make them English. It would be useful to us that way today, when we have poured in upon us, from every direction, influences which are contrary to the traditional views and hopes of our people. It is on the character of our people that this nation will be built, and the character consists of very simple things: earnestness in our work, honesty and truthfulness.'

In the Deerpark Hotel in Charleville, they have their own little exhibition: a print of the scene in the GPO in 1916 beside a photograph of the shopping centre in Charleville, Australia.

The first time a helicopter ever landed at Bruree was on a Sunday evening in July 1966. Not one but two of the great whirling machines descended from a clear blue sky on to Knockmore Hill, one carrying the President of the Republic, the other containing his bodyguards. For Lorcain O'Maonaigh, a local farmer and veteran member of the Eamon de Valera Cumann of Fianna Fáil, it was a day to remember. His daughter Maire was four at the time and he arranged for her to present the President with a bunch of flowers.

Dev, he says, was both pleased and amazed that a little girl from Bruree would be able to speak such good Irish as Maire could. The memory is a source of great pride to him, a part of his firm belief that 'apart from politics altogether, Dev was a great man, a wonderful type of person.' It is one of the things that has kept him loyal to Fianna Fáil through all the decades of change.

The other thing is the memory of an empty house. Lorcain was a young man when his uncle took him to see the house over the Cork border. It was in the house that a brother of Lorcain's mother was killed, along with three other men during the Tan War. The men were having a meeting of the local IRA Brigade when the Tans attacked and shot them out of hand. One of those killed was a young man who had just built the house and was waiting to move into it with his bride-to-be. The house was never lived in again, and it stood there for decades, an admonition and a call-to-arms.

Lorcain isn't sure when he joined Fianna Fáil, since it seemed that he was always in the party. After the Civil War, you always knew which side you had been on, and his family's side was staunchly Republican. 'It wasn't that there was much bitterness or enmity round here, it was just that there was a different sort of relationship. The Fianna Fáil fellas knew each other very well, and the other crowd knew each other very well, and there'd be a different sort of a handshake if you met on the road, that sort of a way.' A man who lived at the end of their boreen used to take Lorcain to Limerick every time that Dev was in town. 'I grew up with all those people, and I never changed.'

That loyalty, though, hasn't been easy. He watched the rise of the Men in Mohair Suits from the sixties onwards with distinct unease. 'I wouldn't go along with 'em now. These men came from a different generation and they probably have a different education, but they'd want to look back to their roots, like. I don't see why they're yapping so much about republicanism if they're short of the whole picture. In the cities, people are different and they come more under outside pressures. You have writers and third-level students and intellectuals and those, and they mean great, but it doesn't all work out either. Charlie's had the divil's own luck – people have come to accept that they have to tighten their belts but you hear of the politicians then going on junkets. I do think that when people move into positions of power, they're often inclined to forget what put them there. I think de Valera was one of the few men who didn't ever forget his roots.

'When I was younger I would go canvassing, but now a lot of the things I thought were important, our people in the party don't bother with. Dev now, when he'd talk, the Irish language would have a priority. He'd always begin his speeches in Irish and go along a good way, and then turn to English. But the people now, I don't know are they Irish or English. It isn't for me to say, I suppose, times are changing.

'Until we get proud of ourselves again, I can't see us doing anything. I see ads on the television and they're advertising books on nature and they're saying "the Book of the British Countryside". That gets me. A lot of our TDs are decent enough people, but they don't seem to think about things. If we want independence we'll have to do something about it, and if not, we might as well sink back into the British world.'

He is not convinced that the party is as serious about a United Ireland as it was in Dev's time. 'I've a lot of regard for Charlie, but Charlie, too, is not altogether a disciple of de Valera's republicanism. A very, very able man, now, and a very human man, but I don't know has Charlie the right mix either. This Anglo-Irish Agreement, for instance, is so vague that both Charlie and Maggie can get something out of it. 'Tis just about better than nothing. A heap of words.' He feels that the violence of the Provisional IRA was inevitable because of the way the Catholics in the North were treated and he had a great deal of sympathy for the H-Block hunger strikers: 'There's a thing about it – you might not agree with these people, but they're your own people, no matter what.

'I think Dev would be fairly disappointed with the party now. But 'tis like Daniel O'Connell. He was regarded as the leader of the nationalist opinion, but the people who came after him didn't think that at all. I suppose you have to live in your own times. If you have a spade and a shovel and no tractor, you have to work with the spade and shovel.'

The image of a man on horseback riding into Bruree playing the fiddle is one that has stayed with Mainchin Seoighe from his childhood. Fiddling away furiously, the horse being led through the village, the whole thing lit by the light of candles in the windows. It was a victory parade, a celebration of Fianna Fáil's triumph in the 1932 election. He had seen de Valera for the first time a few months previously in Kilmallock. 'He came from Newcastle West. There was a great turn-out, a torchlight procession and all the rest of it. I was too young to remember a word of what he said, of course, but the thing that struck me was I thought he spoke exactly as his uncle here in Bruree, Pat Coll, spoke. I would have sworn that it was Pat Coll speaking.'

Pat Coll and Mainchin's mother were neighbours, and later, after he had assumed power, Dev would call sometimes to see her. In 1965, Mainchin spent a day with Dev, taking him around all of the old places. They talked about schooldays, about the pitched battles that the boys from Ballynaught used to fight against the boys from Tankardstown on their way home, about Montecarlo Bergin who got his name from singing *The Man who Broke the Bank at Montecarlo* and used to travel the countryside for Foxy Pat Coll, selling tea from a pony and trap.

Mainchin remains devoted to Dev, is the curator of the de Valera Museum and has written poems in honour of his hero, poems like *The Man From Bruree*:

> *When you honour in song and in story*
> *The men who at Easter uprose,*
> *Who struck for the freedom of Ireland,*
> *And faced the full might of their foes –*

Oh, remember the man from Bruree, boys,
De Valera who answered the call,
He fought in the thick of the battle,
And was last to surrender of all.

Mainchin, too, thinks that Dev might be disappointed at the way both party politics and Irish society have gone. 'Dev was prepared to accept change all right, but I'd say he'd be disappointed at the same time. He'd be somewhat stronger nationally than political leaders are inclined to think now. I think he'd take a firmer stand with Britain than any one of our leaders would now. He would have been pleased at the standard of living and of education that we have now, but I don't know about social change and all these things that are being discussed now.'

'Materialism, the consumer society, wouldn't be his ideal. You see when I was growing up, people round here wouldn't have thought anything strange about comely maidens and all that. It seems to the young people now that that doesn't make sense. But the older people would still believe in the moral order that Dev would have wanted. Society is so open now, with television and media and that, and young people are immature. There certainly seems to be a deviation from old standards. I grew up in the hungry thirties and the isolation and, I suppose, insulation of the war years. Money was scarce, and we had none of the luxuries or amenities of modern life, but people were happier, certainly more contented than they are now. With advertising and everything now, young people's aims are set too high.'

Politics in Bruree is more about getting the vote out than it is about persuading people to vote the right way. Persuasion has little to do with a political landscape whose contours were set down nearly 70 years ago. Padraig O'Liathain, another long-standing member of the Fianna Fáil Cumann in Bruree, says that you can still point to each household in the area and say how they will vote in an election. 'Even to the present day, you'd know the families. Such a family is Fine Gael and such a family is Fianna Fáil. I have never known families to change their allegiance, even going back to their grandfathers. The families are still loyal to the parties that their ancestors and forebears fought for. You can estimate the vote, and in a general election, you wouldn't be out much. You wouldn't hit it head on, but you'd be within a couple of per cent anyway.'

Even getting the vote out isn't as much of a task as it used to be. 'In the early years, transport wasn't as plentiful and that was the problem. Up to the 1960s, there'd be two cars out in this area operating a shuttle service all day long. The Lemass era changed all that – now there's only one or two people who don't have their own transport.'

Padraig's mother's people were very active in the War of Independence and when he was sixteen and wandered into a Fianna Fáil Cumann meeting by accident, he joined up on the spot. That was thirty years ago. 'Dev's first cousin, Mrs Maher, taught me at school, and we'd been hearing of Dev, little stories about him, old people that he knew. His name was a household word. There was fierce loyalty to Dev. No matter what Dev did or what he said, didn't matter. He was right, always right. It was never questioned. Now everything is questioned. Dev led and everyone followed. Nowadays, even if you're a party supporter, you question what the party are doing.'

His own period of questioning was when Fianna Fáil was led by Jack Lynch. 'I have strong feelings on the North, and they'd be very traditionalist. I don't think unity will come overnight – it will be step by step, and I think the Anglo-Irish Agreement is only a tiny step on the road to unity, but come it must. I think the party did lose the nationalism for a while during the sixties and early seventies, they did stray a bit, but I think since Charlie became leader they have come back a little bit again.'

He is, he says, 'against violence and murder', but 'I wouldn't isolate the IRA and say that the IRA alone are committing those atrocities – the British Army is doing it too, along with the militant Unionists. There's no easy answer. I would like to see Sinn Fein brought back into the political process, and I wouldn't support Section 31 either. It's a crazy situation, I think that if they have something to say, let them say it, and let people decide.'

Like all of the Fianna Fáil Cumann in Bruree, Padraig was against divorce, but he thinks it might come in a United Ireland. 'Maybe when talks are held on the unification of the country, maybe then that would be the time to make allowances.' But he doesn't believe social attitudes have changed around Bruree, anyway: 'Moral standards are the same as they have always been. We'd be leading a different kind of life from cities and towns. In a rural area, everyone knows everything about everyone else. You can't be a Jekyll and Hyde character. No matter what you do, it's common knowledge. That helps to keep people on the straight and narrow.'

Next Friday, as he has done for each of the past twenty-five years, Padraig will be heading for the Ard Fheis in Dublin, with at least one or two members of his family. 'At first, it was in the Mansion House, where the crowds were smaller and the atmosphere was more intimate. But even now you make a lot of friends there, you meet the same people year after year – it's more a social event than anything, with a lot of fringe happenings and functions. It's more a holiday weekend than a political event – I have an aunt in Blanchardstown and we stay there. I would go to some sessions of the Ard Fheis, but certainly not them all. I'd always go on a Saturday night for the leader's speech, of course. But most of the time would be spent going round in the vicinity of the RDS – the Burlington or Jury's or the social events in the hall itself.'

Whatever happens this year for Padraig it is unlikely to match the year in the mid sixties when he was up for the Ard Fheis. He called to Aras an Uachtarian to ask if he could leave a photograph for Dev to sign. 'I just called to the gate of the Aras, no appointment or nothing. My mother was with me and my five-year-old son. I told the guard at the gate my business. He rang the house. Dev told the man to let us on in. We were ushered into the waiting room. Then we went into the study and sat opposite him. He spoke a lot about Bruree, families that he knew, trees and bushes that he remembered, the countryside and the simple life of the people.'

This year, at the Ard Fheis, Padraig will be near to the building site which he will not recognise. On it the most expensive group of houses to be built in Dublin this year – set to cost between £275,000 and £300,000 each – are being erected. The site is the former home at Cross Avenue of the Man from Bruree, Eamon de Valera.

1989

Scenes from the Death of the National Movement

In July 1997 Charles Haughey, former leader of Fianna Fáil, admitted that he had received £1.3 million from a businessman between 1987 and 1992.

A decade ago, shortly before he returned to power for his third stint as Taoiseach, Charles Haughey presented a programme called *My Ireland* for Channel 4. Full as it was of sentimental clichés dressed up in high-sounding abstractions, it nevertheless offered the odd glimpse of a deeper truth. One came in a sequence of the Great Helmsman at the wheel of his yacht, the Celtic Mist, metaphorically steering the ship of state through rough winds and high swells. In the voice-over, he spoke as if he were God: 'When the storm sweeps in from the Atlantic and the sea rages with awesome power, one feels very close to the centre of creation.' He talked about the O Dalaigh brothers, the last inhabitants of what is now his private island of Inishvicillaun, the wise old men who initiated him in the lore of the Gael and 'taught us about island life'.

For a moment, the extraordinary fact that a career politician owned an island and a yacht, that he had become inexplicably wealthy, was obscured in a fog of folksy nostalgia and statesmanlike poses. And then his son Ciaran put his hand on the wheel of the boat. 'Don't touch my wheel,' barked the statesman. 'Don't you dare touch my wheel.' The remark was meant, presumably, as self-mockery. But it came across as much less ironic and much more honest than everything that had gone before. For the two concerns expressed in those few words –

power and possession – seemed much closer to the essence of Charles Haughey than all the posturing that had gone before.

And a second sequence was, in retrospect, even more bizarrely eloquent. Again, Charles Haughey was flaunting his possessions. At a racecourse, he talked about his ownership of horses and the fun of seeing them run in his very own colours. Then a figure in a ten-gallon hat, the actor Larry Hagman, famous around the world for his portrayal of the flamboyantly corrupt businessman J. R. Ewing in *Dallas*, approached the Fianna Fáil leader and shook his hand. After some banter, Hagman put his hand in his inside pocket and took out a piece of paper which he presented with a flourish and a leer to the once and future Taoiseach. As the camera zoomed in, we could see what the piece of paper was – a dud thousand-dollar bill with the face of J. R. Ewing on it.

It was like a scene from some bad over-the-top satire, expressing in crude caricature a common perception of Charles Haughey as the kind of shady politician who would take money from an archetypal dodgy businessman. Yet here it was, not an invention but a piece of fly-on-the-wall documentary realism. And it was being presented, not by some scurrilous subversive, but by Haughey himself.

Watching Haughey exhibit his wealth so openly on the programme, you realised that the display itself was a critical aspect of his survival. For he had mastered over many years the difficult art of hiding in plain sight. Instead of seeking to conceal the scandalous truth that he had accumulated greath wealth from what was supposedly a life of public service, he had made it so obvious that it became simply an accepted aspect of Irish reality.

And of course, he himself exercised a significant degree of control over that reality. Because of the libel laws, and his cultivation of a culture of secrecy, Haughey's wealth could only be spoken about in code, and serious attempts to examine its origins, like Frank McDonald's book *The Destruction of*

Dublin, were effectively suppressed. Unlike his successor Albert Reynolds, Haughey always understood that power in an open society is dissipated by crude attempts to enforce it. He rarely threatened legal action. But his power was all the more effective for being restrained. The limits of what could be said were never spelt out, but everyone knew that they existed.

So his wealth became at the same time entirely open and utterly mysterious. It could be seen but not spoken about, observed but not explained. Like the weather or the internal combustion engine, we took it for granted without ever knowing how it really worked.

It is a trick that can only be pulled off when it is not consciously a trick at all, when it arises from deep personal conviction. And this is what is now most obvious about Charles Haughey's naked display of unexplained wealth. He flaunted it because, in his own eyes, he had a right to it. So deeply did he believe in his own greatness that it seemed simple justice that he should have whatever he wanted. He could act so shamelessly because in the world that he had constructed, he had nothing to be ashamed of.

Some indication of the depth of that conviction was given by his evidence at the beef tribunal, the first time he was forced to answer questions about his relations with a wealthy businessman, in this case Larry Goodman. Less than five years ago, Charles Haughey answered questions in the same place and before many of the same lawyers he will face next week. He had retired by then, but he was still, patently, The Boss. He swept into Dublin Castle like a potentate surrounded by his minions, and he made no real effort to disguise the disdain he felt for the petty people who imagined, in their folly, that they could hold him to account.

Under cross-examination, he was, by turns, languidly contemptuous and thunderously indignant. He dismissed some central (and accurate) allegations as not amounting 'to a row of beans'. 'I wonder', he sneered, 'what we're all doing here.' He described other questions about his conduct of public policy as mere 'details' which it would be 'absurd' to expect a man of his stature to be concerned with. In response to one mildly critical question from Eoin McGonigal SC (ironically his own barrister in the present proceedings), his eyes withdrew behind their hooded lids like stoats watching for the kill, and he spat out the words 'I won't have it. I won't listen to it.'

No one watching could believe that this was a mere performance. What we saw then was a consummate show of invincibility, anger and contempt springing from a profound assurance of his own invulnerable power. The authority of the Catholic Church may have been dealt a stunning blow a few months earlier with the revelation of Bishop Eamonn Casey's relationship with Annie Murphy. The mystique of Fianna Fáil itself may have been fatally undermined by Mary Robinson's victory over Brian Lenihan in the 1990 presidential election. Stray pieces of Haughey's own past – most notably his involvement with Sean Doherty in the tapping of journalists' phones – may have already returned to haunt him. But over those few days on which he gave evidence to the beef tribunal every word, every gesture of Charles Haughey's marked him as the last of the untouchables.

It was not hard to guess at the sources of his bitter impatience at being called to account and his supreme confidence that he would emerge unscathed. Had he not leaped over every grave dug for him in the previous thirty years? He had beaten the rap in the arms trial. He had, with astonishing resilience, returned from the political wilderness to lead his party. He had headed off all internal challenges, forcing his enemies into retirement or exile from Fianna Fáil. He had pulled off the most astonishing strokes, hammered out the most unlikely deals, evaded responsibility for the most outrageous scandals.

As his political epitaph he had chosen on his last day as Taoiseach a line from *Othello*: 'I have done the State some service.' But he might more appropriately have chosen one from another Shakespearean tragedy, *Antony and Cleopatra*: 'Comest thou smiling from the world's great snare uncaught?' For until very recently the answer to that question was an emphatic 'yes'. He had passed through a forest of snares, if not quite smiling, then certainly uncaught. Irish society may just about have outgrown Charles Haughey by then, but it had not caught up with him, and it seemed that it never would.

Now that he has been snared, the gulf between his rhetoric and his reality is breathtaking. A man whose love of abstract grandiloquence did not preclude petty, self-serving and bare-faced lies. A man who almost wept when talking of his devotion to the institutions of the State and then thought little of treating a tribunal of inquiry established by both houses of the Oireachtas with contempt. A man of infinite pride without sufficient self-respect to keep him from common beggary. A self-proclaimed patriot whose spiritual home was in the Cayman Islands. A lover of his country who could treat it as a banana republic. A man who called for sacrifices from his people but was not prepared to sacrifice one tittle of the trimmings of wealth and luxury to the cause of preserving the dignity of the State he professed to love. A man who in his Channel 4 film could declare himself 'perhaps a little sentimental, even romantic, in my loyalties to people', and then privately sneer at an 'unstable' friend who had just given him a gift of £1.3 million.

That he was a vulgar, brazen hypocrite is undeniable. But in contemplating the gulf between the rhetoric and the reality it is well to remember that there was also a deeper continuity. 'Deep down', as Haughey told John Waters in the famous *Hot Press* interview, 'I'm a very shallow person.' And this, too, was a moment of truth, for the shallowness of a man on the make and the sonorous depths of his mystical rhetoric were always interdependent.

It is easy to forget the ludicrous extremes of Haughey's self-importance. This is a man who, in *My Ireland*, could emerge from the passage tomb in Newgrange, look into the camera, and speak words written for him by the poet Anthony Cronin as if he had just thought of them himself. 'Malraux claimed that all art came from a desire to defy our nothingness.' This is a man who could, in 1986, send out custom-printed Christmas cards identifying himself with the sea eagle ('Lonely Ruler of the Great Cliffs', 'uncrowned kings of their domain') which he hoped to breed on Inishvicillaun.

This is a man who loved to be photographed on horseback like a warrior knight, and who was willing to have the potted biography introducing his collected speeches claim that his 'descent can be traced back to the Ui Neill, Kings of Ulster. Haughey in Irish means a horseman or knight as the Irish version Eochaidh is derived from the word "Each" meaning a steed. The numerous O hEochaidh clan inhabited a wide area of Mid-Ulster and were Kings of Ulidia up to the end of the 12th century.' And why should not the descendants of knights and kings live in mansions? Why should they not expect tribute from their followers?

Charles Haughey always tried to present himself as an embodiment of Ireland itself. He was careful to make the most of his geographically diverse background, as a man born in Connaught of Ulster parentage, living in Leinster and possessing an island home in Munster. 'Look at the dilemma I'm in,' he tells his family in *My Ireland*, over breakfast on the morning of the all-Ireland semi-finals. 'Of the four teams in it, three of them are Dublin, Kerry, Mayo. I was born in Mayo, I live in Dublin, and I have my holidays in Kerry.' A few moments later, he appeared in Swatragh, County Derry: 'As a child I used to have my holidays here.' Spreadeagled like this between the four green fields, he could mythologise himself as the living image of a dismembered country made whole, of the divisions between north and south, east and west, city and country, somehow healed in the mystical body of our great leader.

The point of all the self-conscious myth-making, all the heroic posturing, was that, in its own way, it served less as a cover for the crass venality of the man than as a justification for it. The inflated self-image provided the excuse for his flagrant self-enrichment. He convinced many people, including presumably himself, that he was a man of destiny. And such men deserve – in their own eyes and those of their faithful followers – the very best. Men of destiny do not live in semi-detached houses. They do not worry about taxes. They convince themselves that the people expect them to live in style, that the gracious life they lead is a compliment to the people they represent.

And the awkward truth is that a very significant proportion of the Irish people did accept Haughey's opulent lifestyle as a compliment. For if his attempts to embody a mystical Ireland were merely ludicrous, he did effortlessly embody a certain kind of real Ireland. It was not the one he tried so hard to evoke, not the misty isle of ancient traditions. It was the more tangible, more vulgar, more human Ireland that emerged from the First Programme for Economic Expansion and began to take shape in the 1960s.

In his maiden speech to the Dail in May 1958, Charles Haughey was careful to touch the right buttons of traditional Fianna Fáil rhetoric, and half of his words could have been spoken by the then party leader Eamon de Valera. He spoke of the need for a 'crusading spirit' in the land and of the party's desire to launch a 'tremendous national crusade'. But he also spoke in a completely different tongue, a language of capital and foreign investment and the making of money. And he came up with a startling definition of 'the trouble with this country'. What was wrong with Ireland, he told the Dail, was not partition, or emigration, or godless American movies, or degenerate jazz dancing, not any of the litany of acceptable ills, but the fact that too few people were getting rich. 'I should like to put forward the proposition that the trouble with this country is that too many people are making insufficient profits.'

On its own, the idea that the making of money is a good thing was not especially remarkable. It is the kind of statement that any pro-business politician might have made then or since. But what was particular about Charles Haughey was that he combined it with an almost religious mysticism. The hard inglorious pragmatism of creating as much wealth as possible by any means necessary was surrounded with a mystical ideology of land and nation, faith and destiny. While his father-in-law Sean Lemass had punctured the inflated rhetoric of de Valera with the sharp edge of economic reality, Haughey did something quite different. He sought to combine Lemass and de Valera, to insert the new vocabulary of maximum profit into the old language of idealistic prophecy.

In this, he was, for the survival of the established political system, a necessary figure. He is a central figure in the creation of modern Ireland because the new direction charted by Lemass and T. K. Whitaker in 1958 needed the support of a national consensus. A simple break with all the old rhetoric, all the accepted pieties, would have been too traumatic, would have risked too much instability. There was room for a transitional figure, for someone who could project the abstract but powerful ideals of nationalism on to the big screen of international modernity. For someone, even, who could suggest that you could devote yourself to getting and spending money and still be a real Irish person, still be a patriotic citizen of what he liked to call 'this unique part of the western world'. Charles Haughey filled that space and became, in the process, one of the architects of the way we live now.

In his performance of this role, it made some kind of sense that he should also live out the national dream in his own life. The conspicuous consumption of the men in mohair suits may have been offensive to many who still believed in the old idealism, but it worked as a kind of metaphor for social and economic change. The rising tide did not lift all boats, but here, at least, was one man who had risen from humble origins to take his place at the wheel of his very own yacht.

The political leaders of that change were offering themselves as role models for the nation. If the trouble with Ireland was that too many people were making insufficient profits, personal enrichment could be imagined as a kind of political solution. Transforming yourself, as Charles Haughey did, from lower-middle-class kid into evident millionaire, could almost be seen as a patriotic duty. Greed, in this ideology, really was good.

Because Haughey talked in the same speeches about the Spirit of the Nation and the making of money, the national ideal and the creation of wealth, it was a short step to begin to believe that the two were part of the same thing. The messianic sense of destiny easily over-rode small-minded concerns about ethics, legality and morality. The line between what was good for some favoured individuals and what was good for the nation as a whole blurred into invisibility.

The new Ireland needed houses – so what if his friend, the property developer and speculator Patrick Gallagher who provided many of them, subsequently turned out to be a convicted crook? Development was part of the nation's destiny – so what if the property deal for the Telecom site, orchestrated by his associate Dermot Desmond, involved a State company paying millions over the odds? Making profits was the solution to Ireland's ills – why should not Pino Harris make £1.75 million on the sale of the Carysfort site to UCD which was 'force-fed' with State funds to make the purchase?

The accumulation of fortunes was in the national interest – why should not the government, at the personal direction of Charles Haughey, break the law in order to meet the financial demands of Larry Goodman? And why, in the natural order of things, should not a small slice of this bounty find its way on to the plate of the leader who had made it all possible?

Nor was all of this just a personal foible, for much as Fianna Fáil would like to distance itself from Haughey, the fact is that his habit of mind was deeply ingrained in the party itself. In its own ideology, Fianna Fáil is the temporal wing of a spiritual entity. The first line of its constitution says that 'Fianna Fáil is a

National Movement' and only subsequently goes on to state that 'The movement shall be organised and known as Fianna Fáil The Republican Party'. Just as the catechism taught us that a sacrament is the outward sign of a state of grace, so Fianna Fáil as a party is the outward sign of an inner state of political grace.

If you are not an ordinary political party then you don't have to play by ordinary rules. You don't have to give the game away about whose interests you really represent. By attaching yourself to a beautiful abstraction like the Nation, you can be on everybody's side, the rich and the poor, the farmer and the urban worker, and whatever you're having yourself. In his now famous 1981 Ard Fheis address, Haughey told the faithful in strikingly religious terms that they got the support of the people because Fianna Fáil 'represents not this pressure group or that sectional interest, this class or that creed, but because in the broad sweep of its membership and their faith and devotion to their own country, there resides what one can well call "the spirit of the nation"'.

The Spirit of the Nation does not need to apologise or explain. The party does not justify itself to the people, is not accountable, because it is the people, or at least the people who matter, the real Irish people. 'This Ard Fheis', Haughey told his congregation in 1984, 'speaks with the authentic voice of Irish Ireland.' And for a long time, this authentic voice of Irish Ireland could be merged with P. J. Mara's Una Voce, Uno Duce.

As Ray Burke declared in 1982 during one of the internal heaves against Haughey: 'Loyalty to Fianna Fáil is loyalty to the nation itself and its social and economic progress.' And since loyalty to the party was loyalty to its leader, then disloyalty to the person of Charles Haughey was an act of treason against the nation. Asking awkward questions about Haughey's role in the connections between business and politics was anti-Irish, unpatriotic. It was, in the words used by Haughey himself about Barry Desmond's attempts to raise frauds by Goodman International in the Dail, national sabotage.

Bertie Ahern this week described the fall of Charles Haughey as 'tragic'. There is a thread of truth in the word, for the protagonists of tragedies are usually figures caught between an old world and an emerging one. Haughey did genuinely represent a period of transition between the death of nationalist Ireland and the painful gestation of an open capitalist economy.

But 'tragic' is also too big a word, for the aspect of that transition that he represented best was the cynicism and opportunism that flourish when one set of values is collapsing and another has not yet been created. Tragedies need heroes, and the only thing heroic about Charles Haughey is the scale of his hypocrisy. What we see in the huge gap between what he was saying and what he was doing is not a compelling human drama but an awful emptiness. It is the moral vacuum that Irish economic success has not been able to fill.

Haughey's fall is painful, not because a man who has had so much power deserves any sympathy, but because the rest of us have to take stock of the fact that we live in a society that has been partly shaped by such a man. We are reminded of just how badly our public and social morality has lagged behind our economic progress. We are forced to look again at the history of the last thirty years, to wonder what seedy deals, what shabby bargains, have determined the direction of public policy. Whatever smugness we may feel about our success in joining the modern world is shaken. If the shock of his disgrace forces us to see the flaws in what we have become in his time, Charles Haughey may, at last, have done the State some service.

1997

Scenes from the Birth of
a New Morality

1.

November 1994. A Catholic priest, Father Brendan Smyth, has been convicted in Belfast of sexually abusing children. Chris Moore's television documentary has revealed that Smyth's career of crime had lasted since the 1950s, and that he had been shielded by the Church authorities. The head of the Irish Catholic Church, Cardinal Cahal Daly, had known of some of Smyth's offences before his arrest, but failed to call in the police.

Anyone with half a heart listening to Cardinal Cahal Daly on RTE's *This Week* radio programme last Sunday would have felt real sympathy for the man, when he confessed that the child abuse scandal currently unfolding had brought him beyond the brink of tears. It is not easy for men to cry, and it is even harder for public men of the Cardinal's generation to talk openly about the shedding of tears.

For a man who carries such a weight of public authority, and who has learned over many years in the cockpit of violent confrontation to be guarded in expressing his feelings, the sudden revelation of those emotions was dramatic. Dramatic but appropriate – for it acknowledged, in a way that more abstract language could not have done, the sheer scale of the crisis that faces both the Catholic Church and Dr Daly himself.

The trauma of the case of Father Brendan Smyth and his forty-year career of paedophilia is immeasurably deepened by the fact that the case itself, in a sense, reveals nothing. A revelation is stunning and unexpected. It alters the known shape of reality.

But the Smyth case is more a confirmation than a revelation. Rather than changing what we know about reality, it confirms it. It puts a face to the dark, faceless knowledge that has clung to Irish childhood for generations. It names a nameless truth.

At the level of raw experience, hundreds of thousands of people in Ireland have known for most of their lives that there is a problem of paedophilia within the Church. Ask anyone who attended a boy's school in Ireland and they will tell you that while most of the teachers were decent and professional there was always one brother or priest who was regarded as a bit of a menace.

The risk of being molested was taken for granted. Because of corporal punishment, the normal rules of acceptable behaviour on the part of adults in authority were understood to be suspended once you went through the school gates. Being beaten and being molested were not from the child's point of view, fundamentally different risks. If the adult world permitted one, there was no reason to believe that it would object to the other.

But to this general knowledge has been added in recent years a growing body of first-hand testimony of much more serious abuse in residential institutions run by the Church. There was Mannix Flynn's account in *Nothing to Say* of his time in Letterfrack Industrial School. There was Paddy Doyle's account in *The God Squad* of his period in an industrial school. Doyle recalled the mixture of brutality and cajoling, distorted sexuality so typical of child abuse, in his case visited on him by a nun who ran the institution.

Perhaps most disturbing of all is Patrick Touher's memoir of his life in Artane Industrial School, *Fear of the Collar*. Touher's account is particularly disturbing because it is written by someone who, unlike Doyle or Flynn, clearly retained a great deal of affection for the Christian Brothers, for the institution and for the Church.

One day, he and two classmates wandered out of bounds to collect conkers. They were caught by one of the brothers. The brother beat the other boys first and then told Touher to come to his room that night. While he was waiting, the other two boys told him that the brother had molested them while beating them. That evening Touher, then aged nine, went to the brother's room. He was stripped, beaten, molested, whipped, and then molested again, the brother promising, 'I'll protect you, I promise, I will never beat you again. I will be like a father to you.'

These three books were published in 1983, 1988 and 1991. They were about the past, and nobody, neither Cardinal Daly nor anyone else, can undo the past. But what those in authority can and should do is to try to make sure that the past remains the past, that the suffering inflicted on innocent children in the 1950s and 1960s would alert the Church to the dangers of the 1980s and 1990s. For even if it were possible that the Church authorities were not aware of the presence of paedophiles and abusers within their ranks before, they could not, after the publication of these grim testimonies, claim ignorance now.

Instead, the knowledge that child abuse within the Church was a long-term and widespread fact of life, known but not acknowledged, seems to have had the opposite effect. If the case of Father Brendan Smyth had been isolated, there is little doubt that the Church would have dealt with it effectively and quickly. But because it was a tangible symptom of a much larger malaise, there seems to have been a sense that it was best not to make an issue of it, lest the issue become an unbearably big one.

In this context, it is easy to understand and to feel personal sympathy for the grief of Cardinal Daly. But it is also important to remember that the Cardinal is not, in this story, just a private figure or even a spiritual leader. He is also the leader of an organisation which holds, and insists on its right to hold, huge temporal power on this island. In particular he is the leader of an organisation which claims wide-ranging rights over the education and welfare of children.

As a private man he is entitled to sympathy. As a spiritual leader he is entitled to respect. But as the wielder of temporal power, he is subject to the same kind of social accountability as anyone else in a similar position. And so far, he has given a poor account of his stewardship in this affair. It is not good enough that he should give a bureaucratic explanation about the chain of command, and his own inability to intervene in the affairs of the Norbertine Order. The trust that Father Smyth played on and betrayed was trust in the Church, not in the Norbertines. Passing the buck down the line like any cornered politician will not restore that trust.

Cardinal Daly's own tears should tell him that the scale and depth of this problem cannot be brushed aside with the language of the bureaucrat or the politician. This crisis is about fundamental things – power, exploitation, authority. It shows what happens in any institution – political, religious or social – where people are taught to obey without question, to accept orders, to do what they are told out of fear and shame and to keep their mouths shut. If the Church is to show that it is no longer such an institution, it must start speaking more openly and more courageously about the lessons it has learned from these terrible events.

2.

November 1994. The consequences of the Brendan Smyth affair spread from Church to State. The Attorney General Harry Whelehan fails to explain delays in processing a request for Smyth's extradition to the satisfaction of the Labour Party, which pulls out of government. The Fianna Fáil leader Albert Reynolds loses office just at the moment of his greatest triumph, his role in bringing about the short-lived IRA ceasefire.

Early last Thursday, as Ireland was waking to the morning after its wildest political night for decades, I met at Heathrow Airport one of the grand old men of Fianna Fáil. Throughout the upheavals within the party in the 1980s, he was one of those who would appear on television to make announcements, to steady nerves, to reassure the public. Now he was walking along an airport corridor pushing a trolley and shaking his head with an air of unfathomable perplexity.

We spoke for a few minutes, but he couldn't find much to say. He had left Ireland a fortnight ago, leaving behind a government with the largest majority in the history of the state and a Taoiseach on the brink of delivering a historic end to the political violence that has seemed endemic to Irish life for a century. Now he was going back to a collapsed government, a disgraced Taoiseach, and a senior judge under pressure to resign, all against the background of a child abuse scandal involving a Catholic priest. The only thing he could be sure of, he said, was that he was glad he no longer had the job of explaining things.

It was easy to agree. For bizarre as the events themselves had been, what was still more amazing was the fact that, for much of Wednesday, the most fantastic rumours had been believed in Dublin. When the Dail met to debate a motion of confidence in Albert Reynolds the Democratic Left TD Pat Rabbitte rose to allege that there was a letter in the Attorney General's office whose contents would rock the state to its foundations. Between then and the emergence of the rather more prosaic fact that the Attorney General's office had, contrary to the impression given to the Dail by Albert Reynolds on Tuesday, dealt previously with a similar case to the Brendan Smyth one, this claim spawned an extraordinary brood of rumours.

These rumours implicated the very highest levels of both Church and State in scandal, forcing the head of the Irish Church, Cardinal Cahal Daly, to go on television to denounce suggestions that he had tried to interfere with the prosecution of the paedophile priest Father Brendan Smyth as 'absurd'. Wild as many of the rumours were, though, they revealed a deeper truth – that the Irish public was now so alienated from those in authority that it was prepared to believe almost anything. How had such complete mistrust taken hold in what used to be one of the most conservative and deferential societies in Europe?

The Irish novelist Flann O'Brien began his surreal novel *At Swim-Two-Birds* with the announcement that there was no reason why a story should have only one beginning, and that his would have three. The story of a surreal week in Irish politics has at least as many beginnings.

One of them is the revelation in 1992 that the Catholic Bishop of Galway, Eamonn Casey, had fathered a son and had used church funds to pay for his upkeep. The erosion of the authority of the Church since that revelation is one of the ingredients of this week's events. Out of it emerges the most shadowy but nonetheless the most potent figure in the drama, Fr Brendan Smyth, the Catholic priest serving a jail sentence in Northern Ireland for sexual offences against children.

A second beginning is in April 1987, when Albert Reynolds as Minister for Industry and Commerce in a minority Fianna Fáil government led by Charles Haughey began a series of dealings with one of the country's most powerful private citizens, the beef baron Larry Goodman. Between then and late 1989, Mr Goodman received from that government an extraordinary series of benefits, most notably $100 million of export credit insurance for his exports to Iraq. The gradual revelation of these dealings in a three-year public inquiry, which finally reported last August, created the climate of suspicion between Albert Reynolds and his deputy in the coalition government, Dick Spring, in which this week's events unfolded.

The third beginning, and the one in which the issues of Church and State in the other two are brought together, is the infamous X case of 1992. In that case Albert Reynolds's newly appointed Attorney General, Harry Whelehan, took out a High Court injunction to prevent a fourteen-year-old girl, pregnant as a result of rape, from leaving Ireland to have an abortion in England. The X case suddenly brought to attention the hitherto unnoticed fact that the low-profile office of Attorney General was one in which the separate areas of laws, politics, morality and religion could collide with the most dramatic consequences. The X case turned Harry Whelehan overnight from an obscure lawyer into a figure around whom many of the most visceral emotions in Irish life – the deep divisions between conservatives and liberals – converged. It ensured that Albert Reynold's determination to appoint him to the second most senior judicial post in the country, the presidency of the High Court, would not, as such appointments usually are, be a matter for public indifference.

If the story has three beginnings, though, it has one theme – the collapse of authority. Behind the breathtakingly rapid series of events is a slower shift in the nature of Irish society. As Ireland has moved in recent decades from a largely rural and traditional society to a largely modern and urban one, the relationship of its people to power has changed. Quite simply, a young, highly educated and largely urban population is not prepared to accept that the exercise of power in Ireland is none of its business.

That change, though, was seldom obvious. The big monoliths of the culture stayed in place. Fianna Fáil, the party which had been in power for most of the history of the State, stayed in power. The Church which had wielded even greater authority, both spiritual and temporal, for even longer, continued, outwardly at least, to enjoy the faith and trust of a large majority of the population. These apparent continuities, though, hid an essential fact – that the public now regarded its loyalties as conditional on the behaviour of those in power. The problem was that those in power did not grasp this change.

The Church, for its part, failed to understand that the Casey affair was more than a shocking aberration. If anything, Bishop Casey's fall from grace looked by the beginning of this week in November 1994 like a golden memory from an innocent past. On Monday, the three big stories on Irish radio and television news were the political repercussions of the Father Brendan Smyth case; the death of a Dublin priest in a gay sauna (fortunately, two other priests were on hand to give him the last rites); and the conviction of a Galway priest for sexual assault on a young man. What was significant was not that these events had occurred, but that they had come into the public domain. The hypocrisies and failings which had always been present within the Church were now coming into the open.

The failure of the Church to understand what was happening was revealed with stark clarity in the Brendan Smyth affair. What emerged after Smyth's conviction in Belfast this summer was that he had been abusing children in Britain, Ireland and America since the 1950s. Each time he was sent to a parish, whispers of scandal would begin to emerge. Each time, he would be sent back to Ireland, and then posted off to another parish. Over four decades, the Church authorities treated his behaviour as an internal affair to be dealt with by admonition or attempts at medical treatment, not as a criminal matter in which the law of the State should have any remit.

The unspoken, perhaps unconscious, belief that the power of the Church was somehow beyond and above the power of the State comes through most strongly in a letter from Cardinal Daly to the family of one of Smyth's victims in Belfast: 'There have been complaints about this priest before, and once I had to speak to the superior about him. It would seem that there has been no improvement. I shall speak with the superior again.'

The idea that the appropriate people to speak to might be the police rather than the superior of Father Smyth's Norbertine Order does not seem to have occurred to the Cardinal. Even in the 1990s, the Church had not grasped the fact that most Irish people now find such notions of unaccountable authority intolerable. But then neither had the State, or, more precisely, the State's vicar on earth, Fianna Fáil. While Father Brendan Smyth's long career of abusing power and trust was beginning to break the surface of discreet silence, Fianna Fáil's use of power was also coming under scrutiny. The tribunal of inquiry into the beef processing industry was producing tangible, if complicated, evidence of a murky relationship between politics, business and the administration of the State. If the details of Albert Reynolds's central role in the affair were difficult for the public to grasp, the talk of private meetings and secret policies, of large benefits for a powerful businessman in a period of severe cutbacks in public spending, created an atmosphere of mistrust. For the first time, the public was given a glimpse of how decisions are actually made in government departments, and what they saw did nothing to enhance the authority of senior politicians.

Ironically, the peace process itself was part of a wider momentum in the island as a whole, one that is at odds with Albert Reynolds's attempts to use it to avoid accountability. That momentum is towards democracy, and away from all forms of private power, whether it be the brute force of private armies, the subtle hints of senior churchmen, or the discreet intimacies of the Cabinet room. The irony is that Gerry Adams grasped the shift in the public attitude to authority more clearly than either Cardinal Daly or Albert Reynolds did.

Far from damaging the peace process, the events of this week have enhanced it. A new settlement in Ireland will only be possible if ideas like democracy, accountability, consent and trust are given real meaning. This week, both Church and State have been given painful lessons in what those meanings should be.

3.

December 1995. In the fallout from the crisis, Fianna Fáil looks like falling apart.

Seldom in peacetime can a parliament have heard a description of a government in action quite like that which the Attorney

General, Eoghan Fitzsimons, read out in the Dail last Tuesday: 'It appeared to me that the Fianna Fáil ministers were behaving in a very disorganised manner. No one appeared to be in charge. At the meetings I attended, ministers came in and out at will, with some being absent for periods.'

Even more remarkable was the fact that this vision of chaos was conjured up by a long-time party supporter and activist. Eoghan Fitzsimons was once a member of Fianna Fáil's Committee of Fifteen – the trustee, not just of a political party, but of The Spirit of the Nation.

More remarkable still was the fact that this was not a condemnation but a plea in mitigation, the best that could be said about the behaviour of the leadership of Fianna Fáil in the week beginning November 14th last. Far from seeking to deny it, some of those same ministers have embraced this description of their own state of mind with considerable enthusiasm, anxiously claiming confusion, tiredness, and even stupidity as desirable epithets.

Nor was the chaos confined to that fateful week. This week too it has been played out live on screen for the nation's delectation. The Spirit of the Nation has descended into a hell of fear and loathing. In the last few days, we have seen a Fianna Fáil Taoiseach 'categorically' and bitterly reject any suggestion that the former Fianna Fáil Attorney General Harry Whelehan ever set foot in his apartment, as if the very notion were repellent.

We have heard the Fianna Fáil Minister for Justice openly contradict the present Fianna Fáil Attorney General. We have been treated to the extraordinary spectacle of the Government Information Service ringing in to RTE's *Prime Time* programme on Tuesday night to claim that the blame for putting through the estimates for government expenditure last week while Fianna Fáil and Labour were still in negotiation about the formation of a new government lay with Bertie Ahern and not with Albert Reynolds. We have had Ray Burke thundering his denunciations of Albert Reynolds to Charlie Bird.

Fianna Fáil is then, by its own account and on the clear evidence of the behaviour of its own senior figures, in a state of utter disarray. The chaos within the party and the damage done to the reputations of virtually its entire upper echelon are so profound as to prompt a question that would have seemed ludicrous even four years ago. Is Fianna Fáil, one of the world's most successful democratic parties, about to go the way of some of the other great ruling political monoliths – the Italian Christian Democrats, Japan's Liberal Democratic Party, the Communist Party of the Soviet Union, the Congress Party in India – and enter a period of terminal decline?

For Fianna Fáil, the events of the last few weeks, horrendous as they have been, would be much less serious if they were much more like the last time a Fianna Fáil Attorney General dominated the news, when the murderer Malcolm McArthur was found in Patrick Connolly's flat in 1982. That occurrence was genuinely grotesque, unbelievable, bizarre and unprecedented, a wild accident of fate. Those at the top of the party now would like to believe that recent events are of the same order. The very attraction of the idea of confusion, even of stupidity, to those involved suggests that there is for them some bleak form of comfort in the idea that it all happened because of grotesque but unpredictable human failings.

This is, of course, partly because it is better to be judged stupid than corrupt. But it is also a natural reaction to disaster. When a plane crashes into the side of a mountain, it is somehow more comforting to be told that the accident resulted from pilot error than from structural flaws in the aircraft's guidance system. All week, Fianna Fáil's pilot, co-pilot, chief stewardess and maintenance crews have been blaming each other for the disaster. Painful as this is, it is much more pleasant than facing the fact that the machine was not just badly handled but may also have built-in flaws which will prevent it from getting off the ground again.

The hard truth is that what is most remarkable about recent

events is not that they occurred, but that they were so long delayed. Fianna Fáil has been in serious disarray since the trauma of Charles Haughey's coup against Jack Lynch in 1979.

That putsch, and the public bickering within the party ever since, has gradually eroded the very core of Fianna Fáil's appeal – the mystical but powerfully effective charisma of the National Movement.

This powerful ideology has been undermined in recent years by three inter-related forces. One is the long-term and global trend away from monolithic identifications in the kind of complex western society that Ireland has become. A second is the diminishing resonance of the broader cultural symbols that Fianna Fáil drew on – nationalism, Catholicism and the Irish language. The third, and most fatal, is the obvious and naked division within the party itself since 1979. Whatever chance a united, coherent Fianna Fáil might have had of surviving the long-term changes in Irish society intact, a party riven by uncivil wars had none. When the authentic voice of Irish Ireland is in reality a bickering Tower of Babel, it can no longer speak with authority.

Throughout the 1990s, the public has been treated to the most dramatic images of Fianna Fáil at odds with itself. The unceremonious shafting of Brian Lenihan when he became an embarrassment during the 1990 presidential election campaign; the comedy of Gerry Collins's live television appeal to Albert Reynolds not to 'burst up the party'; the ruthless use of hints about Bertie Ahern's private life dropped by Michael Smith and Albert Reynolds himself in the 1992 leadership contest – such moments dispelled once and for all the image of a mystical union by which Fianna Fáil had avoided the need to answer for its actions.

Even worse, with the passing of Charles Haughey, Fianna Fáil no longer possessed a figure capable of sustaining interest in the division of the political world into the elect and the damned, the National Movement and the traitors, on which the party's aura had depended. The idea of Irish politics as a permanent fixture between Fianna Fáil and a World XV was undermined by the coalition with the Progressive Democrats in 1989, and shattered by the coalition with Labour. Fianna Fáil was just another political party, but one whose whole culture denied the need to account for its actions.

What is striking in retrospect about the advent of Albert Reynolds is that those around him were not blind to what was happening to the party. If Albert Reynolds himself lacked perspicuity, his ablest lieutenants Maire Geoghegan-Quinn and Padraig Flynn did not. There is no reason to doubt the sincerity of their public statements in early 1992 about the need to 'let in the light', about a new spirit of openness and about their desire for the party to take a hard look at itself. Whatever their desires, however, they lacked the capacity to fulfil them. In broad terms, Fianna Fáil did not have the intellectual resources to come up with a new ideological direction.

The consequences of these problems were made clear in the dreadful performance of the party in the 1992 election. But for the extraordinary intervention of Dick Spring to save Albert Reynolds by going into coalition with him, the party would have been able to face those consequences in opposition.

Instead, it was placed back in power with all of its fundamental problems frozen in place. Salvaged from the judgement of the electorate, Fianna Fáil was lulled into complacency, forgetting the truths about the state of the party that even Albert Reynolds had acknowledged when he first became leader.

The National Movement has been irreparably destroyed, and the task of re-inventing Fianna Fáil as an ordinary democratic political party is now much more difficult than it was even two years ago. For one thing, Bertie Ahern has to begin that task in an atmosphere of bitter recrimination and with his own reputation and those of almost all of his senior colleagues badly tarnished. For another, the emergence of a strong centre ground consensus in Irish politics, with Fianna Fáil, Labour and Fine

Gael all occupying similar political territory, makes it very difficult to construct a coherent opposition while still maintaining a catch-all appeal. Just as John Bruton found it very difficult in the last two years to find a clear line of attack on the Fianna Fáil–Labour consensus, so too will Bertie Ahern, all the more so since any new coalition will almost certainly be implementing a programme which Fianna Fáil was already committed to in its partnership with Labour. A new leader of Fianna Fáil starting out with a good stock of political capital would find that task formidable. A new leader whose political capital has already been dramatically devalued may well find it impossible.

4.

June 1995. The secret life of Ireland's most famous Catholic priest, Father Michael Cleary, a passionate defender of conservative values until his death in December 1994, has been revealed. He had fathered two children with his 'housekeeper' (in fact his common-law wife), Phyllis Hamilton. Bishop Brendan Comiskey hints that it may be time for a debate on clerical celibacy.

'Gossip', wrote the late Andrew Kopkind, 'serves as justice in a corrupt world.' In a piece about Kitty Kelley's scurrilous biography of Nancy Reagan (included in a terrific recent collection of his writing, *The Thirty Years' Wars*), Kopkind noted that 'In a more perfect place, Nancy Reagan would have been brought to trial for crimes against sincerity, candour and taste, and surely judgement would have been terrible and swift. The United States penal code, however, omits such offences, so there's only Kitty Kelley to even the scales.'

In a more perfect place, too, Father Michael Cleary's lapses of taste, his coarsening effect on Irish public life, his substitution of crude propaganda for reasoned argument would have been more than enough to tarnish his reputation. Instead, we are left with gossip as a pale and inadequate substitute for justice. Yet again, we see the public realm – the arena of social responsibility and political participation – shrink into the private domain of sexuality and property.

Yet again, too, we have to put up with the fantasy that the saga of Michael Cleary has something to do with a confrontation between the media and the Church. The Church's response to anything in the media has now become so automatically one of blank denial that Bishop Brendan Comiskey has to publicly deny the ridiculous claim of Cardinal Daly that the former's remarks on celibacy had been 'taken out of context' in media reports. By blaming the media, the very existence of a real problem and a real debate can be blithely denied.

Equally, Church sources now talk as if Michael Cleary himself had not been, first and foremost, a media personality. He had, lest it be forgotten, a column in the *Sunday Independent* for five years. He then had a column in *The Star*. And he had, for four years, an hour-long, five nights a week phone-in show on 98FM. He was a clergyman in the same sense that the Reverend Ian Paisley is – a man who brings the aura of religious authority into public life.

And in that public life as a journalist and broadcaster, he showed no reluctance to encourage the worst tendencies of tabloid journalism – the conflation of journalism and showbusiness, the substitution of emphatic assertion for verifiable fact, the repetition of paranoid fantasies as public truths. Especially on the most difficult public issue of abortion, he engaged in staggeringly insensitive stunts.

During a televised debate on the 1983 abortion referendum, he made the wildest of connections between the wording of a constitutional amendment and the obliteration of people with disabilities by drawing attention to a young woman in a wheelchair. He later described his own methods of ensuring that the presenter John Bowman introduced this woman into the programme: 'I actually went over to him during a commercial break and I said "If you don't call her, I'm going to push her out in front of the cameras."'

Ten years later, on his radio show, Michael Cleary used the opportunity of an interview with Mother Teresa to make vile allegations about the family at the centre of the X case, saying that the case was 'a model . . . planned deliberately to test the amendment' and that he suspected a great deal of organisation behind it.

This was a grotesque falsehood, made all the worse by the fact that he associated the moral authority of Mother Teresa, who clearly knew nothing about the reality of the X case, with it. It was a vastly more abusive and nastier allegation than anything the *Sunday World* has written about Michael Cleary. It implied the most disgusting conduct on the part, not merely of lawyers, journalists and Supreme Court judges, but much more importantly of an innocent and abused child. By comparison, an allegation that a man fathered children in a consensual and loving relationship, even if it were untrue, pales into insignificance. When it came to giving scandal, Michael Cleary needed no lessons. And if, as Father Cleary's friends now suggest, it is wrong to make allegations against someone who cannot defend himself, how much worse was it to make allegations against a family which could only identify itself by exposing a hurt child to the public gaze?

The point is not that one bad turn deserves another, but that, in his career as a journalist and broadcaster, Michael Cleary is at least as responsible as anyone else for the coarsening of public discourse to the point where we now have a dead man's Valentine cards reproduced in full colour in a national newspaper. And he carried that crudity into his belief that the public good, the political arena, should be defined by people like himself.

When, in the abortion debate, even the Catholic hierarchy was recognising 'the right of each person to vote according to conscience', Michael Cleary was telling priests in his *Sunday Independent* column to 'start this Sunday by telling your people about life and its origins . . . Tell them to vote "yes" and make no apology for it.' Later, after the divorce referendum, he boasted that 'individual priests like myself' made all the running, while 'the bishops were very soft'. The sheer vulgarity of such an approach to political debate, flattening out even the subtleties and complexities of his own Church's position, did a great deal to coarsen public life in Ireland.

Gossip may be rough justice, but in the case of Michael Cleary it may be justice nonetheless, not as an eye for an eye but as a reminder of just why it is so wrong to treat public issues with crass moral absolutism. If it is true that Ireland's best-known priest had a lover and children, it just might convince some people that human realities can never be reduced to mere sloganising. In public, Michael Cleary said things like 'The Church can alter certain regulations and laws that it makes itself, but it can't change the laws of God. We give the maker's instructions and we can't bend them – they're not ours to bend.' In private, it seems, that unbending certainty was abandoned.

What can be abandoned in private should also be abandoned in public. It is not too late in Ireland to create a public realm in which debate is free of paranoia, scandal-mongering and the pulling of religious rank. The courage of Bishop Brendan Comiskey in trying to drag the Church into a new era of calm and open discussion of controversial issues is a good start. But it has been met with the usual conspiracy theories. Cardinal Daly has hinted at 'a campaign' in 'some sectors of the media', referring, I presume, to the Catholic magazine *Reality*, which in its May issue reported a survey of its readers, most of whom are committed Catholics aged over 50 and 63 per cent of whom believe that it is time to end mandatory celibacy for priests. If, in spite of the Cardinal's refusal to see what is in front of his nose, Bishop Comiskey and his allies manage to establish a new kind of public discourse in the Church, they will help to create an atmosphere in which justice will not need gossip to do its dirty work for it.

5.

August 1995. An abandoned baby is buried on the west coast of Ireland.

On Wednesday morning, a child was buried in the churchyard in Waterville, County Kerry, under a gravestone marked 'Finian', in honour of the local saint. He was a little boy, found dead on the strand by a local man and his son, out for an early morning walk. The funeral had been arranged by the Garda and the priest, the representatives, if you like, of State and Church, the big powers of Irish society disposing of the anonymous child of an anonymous and unknown mother and father.

Ten years ago, such a scene would have been a metaphor for all that was despicable about Irish society. Then, a burial like that of baby Finian could only have been seen through the blood-tinted spectacles of the Kerry Babies inquiry which had taken its final submissions a few weeks earlier. Finian would have reminded us all of the baby boy found in similar circumstances in April 1984 on White Strand, just a few miles from Waterville.

The discovery of that baby, of course, had led to a bitterly shameful episode in which an innocent woman was charged with murder, and four members of her family were charged with concealing the birth of an unnamed male child. This in turn led to a protracted public inquiry that descended, as the Garda put forward increasingly bizarre theories to justify their behaviour, into the grotesque, with the woman who had been the victim in the affair becoming the object of hysterical slander.

121

The Kerry Babies episode became not just an exposure of religious hypocrisy and State incompetence, but itself a shameful symptom of a society's sickness.

Yet, if it is a metaphor at all, the burial of baby Finian on Wednesday is one with a very different meaning. The fact that there are still dead babies in the beaches and fields of Ireland – there have been similar incidents in Listowel and Drimoleague this year – reminds us, indeed, that for all the talk of a brave new Ireland, there is still a strong current of fear and shame beneath the apparently calm surface of our morality. But within that awful continuity, the change in attitudes could hardly be more profound.

It is now obvious, however tacitly, that Irish society no longer treats the death of an abandoned infant as a crime requiring prosecution and punishment. On *Morning Ireland* on Wednesday morning, a Garda made it clear that the force's only concern in trying to trace the mothers of such babies is to make sure that they are getting the necessary medical and psychological help and to 'close the book' on the investigation. In the case of the Listowel and Drimoleague babies, this has been done.

In the case of baby Finian, the burial was held off for weeks in the hope that the mother might come forward and that her own wishes for the funeral might be respected. The name on the gravestone and the place of burial have been widely broadcast, so that the mother, whether or not she ever chooses to come forward, may in the future be able to visit the grave. These are basic courtesies, but in a society where until quite recently unbaptised infants were buried in unmarked graves in unconsecrated ground between sunset and sunrise, they are eloquent evidence of something that it is often hard to notice: that Ireland is becoming a more civilised place.

The striking thing about these new attitudes on the part of State and Church is that, in spite of all the bitter divisions in Ireland on issues of personal morality, it would be hard to find anyone to stand up and say that the Garda are showing a disgracefully lax attitude to the law, or that women who actively or passively contribute to the deaths of their infants should in fact be prosecuted and punished. Instinctively, anyone who is not a complete crank knows that morality and respect for the law are enhanced rather than undermined by the merciful compassion that is now shown to women in these circumstances.

And yet, even though almost everyone agrees that this is the case, almost everyone is equally loath to say on what grounds this should be so, or to spell out the general principles that make it right. What we have, after all, is a deliberate and apparently systematic policy of not applying the law. Under the Infanticide Act of 1949, a woman suspected by the police of having killed her baby should be charged with murder. Equally, a parent who neglects or abandons a child commits a serious criminal offence. So what does it tell us when we think it right that these serious laws should be effectively and publicly placed on one side?

It tells us, I think, two very important things, each of which has an important bearing on the development of a society that is both civilised and pluralist. The first is that people can be better than the law, that we need to stop thinking of the law of the land as the be all and end all of our morality. The second is that, when it comes to the big issues of life and death, we are much more decent, and much more sophisticated, than we give ourselves credit for.

Social conservatives take an essentially pessimistic view of the relationship between the way people behave and the way the law says they should behave. They believe that the law should set a very high but immutable standard for behaviour. They know, of course, that many people will fall short of this standard but they think that, if the standard were lowered or removed, we would go to the dogs altogether. They therefore argue that, however many 'hard cases' there may be, it is better to keep the law in place and to see it through.

Yet the profound change in the way we treat abandoned babies and their mothers utterly contradicts this notion. The effective suspension of the law, far from making for more bad behaviour, has made us, as a society, behave infinitely better than we did even a decade ago. Though it should not have taken the burning at the stake of Joanne Hayes to make it happen, the fact is that we do now behave with more compassion, more sensitivity, more tenderness towards hurt women. We behave, in other words, more morally. We have discovered in at least one area of Irish life – a very difficult and traumatic one at that – that less law can mean more morality.

Or rather, to be more accurate, this is not so much a discovery as an admission. One of the strange things about Ireland is that, perhaps uniquely among societies, we have insisted on proclaiming a public morality that is in many ways worse than our private values. Our peculiar form of hypocrisy has been not a whitened but a blackened sepulchre, proclaiming to the world a rigid, intolerant, heartless face that belies the actual decency and humanity of the way ordinary Irish people tend to look upon people in trouble. If we can continue to construct laws that reflect our better selves, the new gravestone in Waterville churchyard may serve, not just as a sad memorial to an Ireland we are still trying to escape from, but also as a signpost to a society that could offer a decent home to the likes of little Finian.

6.

November 1995 – the morning after the referendum to remove the prohibition on divorce, the last specifically Catholic clause, from the Irish Constitution.

Dr T. K. Whitaker, one of the prime movers in the creation of modern Ireland, once visited the shrines of Irish saints on the

European continent, among them Saint Gall at St Gallen and Saint Virgilius at Salzburg. He was delighted to find that they shared their altars with local saints – Gall with a Saint Otmar and Virgilius with a Saint Ruprecht. 'I suppose', he joked in a lecture in 1977, 'Irish initiative and devotion needed eventually to be underpinned by German organisation and method!'

It was, if you were opening Ireland to all the uncertainties and discontinuities of the modern world, as Dr Whitaker and Sean Lemass did in the 1960s, a comforting image. On the altar of Catholicism, Irish devotion could sit side by side in mutual comfort with the method and organisation of industrial modernity. The most sweeping changes in politics, the economy and society could be undertaken in the belief that a core of tradition, contained above all within the Catholic faith, would remain unaltered. Change would underpin Irish devotion, not undermine it. Therefore change was not to be feared but to be embraced.

In this sense, religious devotion in Ireland was not the enemy of social change but one of the main things that facilitated it. It provided a layer of continuity that helps to explain why Ireland has coped so well with all the confusion and uncertainty of moving from a very predictable society to a very open and unpredictable one. And perhaps one of the lessons of the divorce debate is that the opposite is also true: that in a time of crisis for the Catholic Church, it is harder, not easier, for Catholics to cope with the idea of change.

Until recently, the relative stability of Irish Catholicism was truly remarkable. While almost everything was changing, the practice of the Catholic faith remained largely intact. Ireland joined the EU and developed a society closely comparable to other European democracies in lifestyles, sexual behaviour and social problems. But over 80 per cent of Catholics in the Republic still attend Mass at least once a week, compared to less than half in Spain and Italy, and less than one in eight in France.

Precisely because Ireland has been changing so rapidly, the Church represented for many people the last bastion of stability and security. Those who favoured social change always saw the church, for obvious reasons, as a barrier to progress. Yet the divorce debate has shown that, even with the institutional church at its weakest for 150 years, there is still massive resistance to change. Whatever the outcome of the vote, this should force everyone to re-think the relationship between religion and politics in Ireland.

The institutional church did, of course, enter the debate with even more determination this time than it did in 1986. Not only were its biggest guns – the Pope and Mother Teresa – trained on the electorate, but the threat of hellfire and damnation was made all but explicit in Bishop Thomas Flynn's warning that divorced people would not be entitled to the sacraments. Liberals would like to believe, if the referendum is lost, that they were defeated by these traditional antagonists.

But all the evidence is to the contrary. Both William Binchy and Des Hanafin of the Anti-Divorce Campaign were embarrassed by Bishop Flynn's intervention. A parish priest in Bruff who instructed primary school pupils to distribute the bishop's pastoral letter on divorce was unanimously condemned by parents and forced to apologise. And only 7 per cent of voters polled by the MRBI for the *Irish Times* stated that they would vote No primarily on religious grounds. What all of this suggests is that Church intervention was at best minimally helpful to the anti-divorce side, at worst counter-productive.

Arguably, indeed, the loss of authority over Irish society by the bishops was a bigger factor in the campaign than their attempts to exercise authority. While many liberals expected the exposure of the bishops in the spate of child abuse scandals to make people more likely to embrace change, it seems in fact to have had the opposite effect.

It needs to be remembered that most Irish Catholics experience the disgrace of their bishops and the loss of trust in their priests not as a liberation but as a trauma. The one thing that seemed stable and trustworthy throughout the breathless decades of change has suddenly become itself full of dark secrets, of terrible unpredictability, and of dreadful ambiguities. Not only are bishops fleeing the country and priests suddenly disappearing from parishes, but the stories that are emerging cast a shadow on the recent past as well as on the present. They are often stories about what happened in the 1960s and the 1970s, and they throw a sickly retrospective light back on what seemed to be a more orderly time. Not just the present but also the past seems suddenly darkened.

The effect is that sincere Catholics are, as Bishop Willie Walsh wrote in the *Irish Times* recently, 'hurt, sad, angered, frustrated, fearful and insecure'. The anger, sparked by the paedophile scandals, may be directed largely at the bishops themselves, but fear and insecurity seldom have the effect of encouraging people to embrace change. The very strong backlash against divorce has shown that many people in Ireland do not share the confidence and optimism about the future that has become almost an orthodoxy in politics and the media.

Some social research has already suggested that this might be so. In a Landsdowne/Henley Centre study last year, two thirds of Irish adults said that there will be more fear in Irish society by the year 2000. Half expected less tolerance, less generosity and a less caring society. Much of this fear can be traced to economic failures: 56 per cent expect higher unemployment, and 71 per cent expect crime and violence to be worse. But the divorce debate suggests that it has even wider dimensions. Fear of social breakdown, fear of losing everything that makes Ireland in any way different from other western societies, fear, above all, that the relationships between people will dissolve if they are not enforced by law – these were the raw nerves that the anti-divorce campaign managed to touch.

Politics has been unable to turn such fears into hopes. For the other thing that the divorce debate has told us in no uncertain terms is that political authority has crumbled even more decisively than has the authority of the Church. The seven largest political parties in the State – Fianna Fáil, Fine Gael, Labour, the Progressive Democrats, Democratic Left, the Green Party and Sinn Fein – all urged a Yes vote. Liberals, paradoxically, believed that the party faithful would do as they were told, and that Fianna Fáil in particular would be able to carry at least the bulk of its supporters with it.

The evidence of every recent by-election, and the bewildering shift in political alliances since the last general election, made that an unlikely proposition. And so it has proved to be. And if that is worrying for political leaders, what should be even more so is that the issue that all of them believe to be of the greatest moment – peace in Northern Ireland – had no discernible influence on the debate. The idea that the peace process has profound implications for the way the Republic conducts itself does not seem to have taken hold. The fundamental belief that political change can make things better seems largely absent at the moment.

With politics in flux and the Church in crisis, the family seems to many people to be the only institution that can offer a refuge from uncertainty. When everything else appears temporary and contingent, there seems to be a deep desire to pretend that family life is insulated against the winds of change. It is because the old order is falling apart that the image of people sticking together, come what may, has such a powerful allure. The temptation to retreat from a confusing and uncertain public realm into a warm image of private family bliss seems, for many Irish people, to be irresistible just now.

Whatever the result of the referendum, therefore, it would be a mistake to see it as a decisive turning point. It will be neither a turning back towards a confident assertion of a conservative and secure Catholic identity, nor a confident step into a new era. The debate has revealed conservatives to be extraordinarily pessimistic about the future, seeing Irish society as so fragile that it could be destroyed by changing a single clause in the Constitution. And it has shown modernisers that their own optimism is contradicted by the existence of a deeply divided and anxiety-riven society around them.

A narrow victory for either side today will leave Irish society in a condition of rather sour stalemate. If the No side wins by a small margin, it will have to reflect that it has seen its dominance very sharply reduced in just nine years, and that it has merely postponed an inevitable change. Moral crusades need to be won by a convincing margin, not to squeak through by a few votes, leaving nearly half the electorate embittered and increasingly alienated from the Church. Equally, if the Yes side wins narrowly, it will do so in the sobering knowledge that nearly half the electorate doesn't share its basic belief that Irish society is getting better. Two cheers may be as much as anyone can manage.

1995

(*The electorate voted, by a tiny margin, in favour of the introduction of divorce.*)

The Man of Your Dreams

Pock. The ball rebounds off the springy, flat wood of the bat and spins through the air towards an open hand waiting to grasp it. The ball is bowled again. *Pock*. It is the sound of high blue skies, airless days and lush, rich greenery but it echoes now off dull unplastered concrete as the ball traces its way through the grey overbearing skies of a Mayo Sunday. The cricketers' brown skin and black, shiny hair stand out all the more against the fierce whiteness of their open-necked shirts, their dark arms sticking out below sleeves that are tightly rolled to just above the elbow. Little boys and their fathers playing together to pass the afternoon, they have no proper stumps, never mind a rolled, even cricket pitch. They toss the ball back and forth over the scrub ground littered with patches of gravel, broken concrete blocks, odd bits of building materials.

Behind them are their own houses, surrounded by a rough wall, facing away from the road as if turning their backs to the small town of Ballyhaunis in which they find themselves. In front of them, up a long tarmacadamed driveway, is a huge hulking new house, its roof as black as their hair, its walls as white as their shirts. The house, which the locals say cost a million pounds to build, could be a hugely inflated version of a normal country house, set as it is next to a stark, open quarry in landscape that looks mean and dishevelled – except that built into its facade are flowing Islamic arches, fantastic and arabesque. They give the house the lightness of a spaceship that has just landed on this alien terrain – that might, at any moment, take off into the overhanging clouds. It is the house of Sher Rafique, the Pakistani businessman who owns much of Ballyhaunis, and whose Halal meat plant employs the greater part of the male workforce.

A few yards down the road, inside the Midas Bar, Restaurant and Nite Club, the drains have to be unblocked, the ashtrays emptied, the broken glasses swept up. The stale smell of last night's dance still has to be exorcised and the rehearsals for tonight's talent contest are already behind schedule. While the cricketers swing luxuriantly, the owner of the Midas Club, Paul Claffey, is a whirl of activity, dragging tables, shunting chairs, doling out orders. 'Get another barrel up . . . check the level on those mikes . . .' In just a few hours, this old dancehall, littered with the lonesome evidence of last night's dissipations, will have to be transformed into a dream factory. Tonight 'Sunday Night Live at the Midas' features both the finals of the Zanussi Entertainer of the Year competition and another instalment of Paul Claffey's own version of the television game show *The Price Is Right*. Tomorrow morning at the factory it may be all sheep's intestines and barrels of blood, but tonight at the dream factory it has to be sheep's eyes and barrels of beer. Already, on stage, a young woman with an enormous Irish harp is practising *The Mountains of Mourne* and there's gangs of Paddies digging for gold in the streets.

Paul Claffey is thirty-four and has been in the entertainment business for nearly a quarter of a century. When he was ten he started running discos in the Marist Brothers school in Castlerea, a few miles across the Roscommon border from Ballyhaunis. During the summer holidays, he and three friends hired sound equipment and ran the disco in the school hall. For their pains, they made twelve shillings each. The other three reckoned that the returns were out of all proportion to the effort and gave up. Paul reckoned that four twelves would be forty-eight and two quid wasn't to be sneezed at, so he carried on on his own.

Shortly afterwards he noticed that there was always a row about whose turn it was to go up the town for Coke and crisps when the lads went to the swimming pool. He took his bike to the local Coke distributor, persuaded him to give him a crate on tick and started his own shop outside the swimming pool. By the time he was twelve, he was hiring function rooms in all the local towns, employing a driver to take himself and the disco gear around. He started booking live acts, bringing them down from Dublin to the dancehalls of the area. He was still so young that he had to pretend to the bands that the Paul Claffey who had booked them was unfortunately indisposed and that he had just been sent along with a message. By the mid seventies he had the leases on five of the biggest dancehalls in South Mayo, North Galway and Roscommon.

What made him was demographics. With a baby boom and very little emigration, there were plenty of young kids around, kids who identified with youth culture and not with country and western or middle-of-the-road cabaret. Paul Claffey spotted the gap in the market and dived in, bringing rock acts like Brush Shields, The Freshmen and even Thin Lizzy to Ballyhaunis and Gort. Almost overnight, Horslips tapped a whole new market for indigenous rock music. Paul Claffey had them booked for £125 to play the Royal Cinema in Roscommon town. In between the booking and the gig, the band broke it big. He made his £125 back on the raffle at the interval.

But the tide of youth began to ebb as the seventies gave way to the eighties. There were fewer young people around as emigration began to edge upwards again. The High Court loosened restrictions on hotels getting bar extensions for cabarets and the dancehall boom was over. In four months, Paul Claffey lost all of his dancehalls and a pub. He was dragged through the courts over matters of money. He had just enough left to risk it all on getting a drinks licence for the old dancehall in Ballyhaunis, now re-named The Midas Club. It cost him £65,000 but he did it. When he opened his doors and the young people who had been his regular customers arrived, they were discreetly turned away. He had decided to go for the family market, the married couples and the middle-aged who had nothing to do on a Sunday night. Round here, there was no future in the young.

Bismillah allahu akbar! The slaughterman is looking down into the upturned face of the sheep. Only the sheep's neck and head stick out from the pen which holds it fast. The sheep enters, the pen closes and revolves, leaving its neck pointing upwards, ready for the blade of the slaughterman. The Koran lays down that an animal must be killed in the name of God and that it must be killed with a sharp knife, without violent blows. The prophet discouraged the eating of too much meat – 'Don't', says the Koran, 'make your stomachs the graveyard of animals' – and those animals which were killed were generally raised by the family and slaughtered with great respect and gravity by the head of the household. Muslims, however, have been eating more and more meat in recent years and the Prophet's injunctions have had to be adapted to industrialised production. In Ballyhaunis, a dozen Muslim slaughtermen – Egyptians, Turks, Syrians, Pakistanis – act as mullahs, muttering the prayer *Bismillah allahu akbar* (In the name of God, God is greater) while they sever with one cut the twin arteries of the throat, cutting off the supply of blood to the brain, causing loss of consciousness and death.

Twelve years ago, when Paul Claffey's dancehall empire was burgeoning, Sher Rafique built a small slaughtering shed by the side of the road, on a one-acre site a few hundred yards outside Ballyhaunis. Now there are ten individual plants on the site and Halal (the name is the Islamic equivalent of kosher) is the biggest exporter of lamb from the country, the second biggest of beef. Sixty per cent of those exports go to the EEC, largely to the big ethnic Islamic market, the rest to North Africa and the Middle East. The plant now straggles half a mile out the road, one virtually unbroken blind wall of concrete. The far side of the road is littered with thousands of pounds worth of building materials: blocks, pipes, shores, posts, all strung out in a line going nowhere. Behind them is Sher Rafique's house and, the frame of its half-built dome naked against the sky, a mosque.

Those who frequent the mosque are never to be seen in the other gathering places of Ballyhaunis. They don't drink, so they don't go into the pubs. They don't dance, so they don't go into the Midas. Aside from the children who attend the local national school, the Muslims are a familiar but largely enigmatic presence. When they eat in the restaurants, they generally want to be served quickly and be away again. Across the road from the entrance of the Midas, a family of Syrians lives, but Paul Claffey doesn't know much about them, except that they are decent, quiet people. It's not that anyone has a bad word to say about the people who increasingly provide the town's reason to exist, or that there is any obvious racism, just that everyone is happy enough for their presence to remain insulated and discreet. Once, one of the Muslim workers wandered into the Midas and asked for some 'white music'. He was given a tape of some Irish country and western and he left, never to return. When their presence does impinge, however, it does so very obliquely. At the Midas talent contest that Sunday evening, it is kept safely at a distance.

Suddenly, from the bank of speakers on the Midas stage, the 'Also sprach Zarathustra' music from *2001* blares out: *daah, daah, da-da*. 'And now, ladies and gentlemen,' announces Paul Claffey, 'with the time at twenty past the hour of ten o'clock, we present the Zanussi Entertainer of the Year final. And here is your host, the one and only John Duggan.' John Duggan has already been on stage an hour before, to introduce Louise Morrissey and her band. Louise has changed out of her jeans and into a silver lamé knee-length suit, the boys in the band have doffed their jumpers and put on their blue cowboy-style suits with knee-length jackets, white shirts, blue dicky-bows and shoes so black and shiny they make pure whiteness look dull. The two young girls who are always the first to take the floor in any dancehall have already danced on their own to *My Tears Have Washed I Love You From The Blackboard Of My Heart*, turning little twirls and pirouettes before being joined by a quickening trickle of dancers for *The Night Daniel O'Donnell Came To Town* and *The Green Glens of Antrim*. The band has already finished its first set and John Duggan has been warning the crowd not to sit in the passageways. 'You'll say to yourself "Wasn't I an awful fool to sit here".' But the one and only John Duggan has to be introduced again, because now the show is being broadcast live on Paul Claffey's own pirate radio station, Mid-West Radio, the signal being beamed to much of Mayo, Galway, Sligo, Leitrim and Roscommon, from a tiny room at the back of the Midas.

John Duggan does the late-evening easy-listening show on Mid-West Radio. He started doing it shortly after the station was established in November 1985. At the time, he had not yet retired from his job and was still serving as a Garda in Glanamaddy. He had been in the guards long enough to remember serving in Crumlin garda station when it was one half of a thatched cottage shared with Saint Agnes GAA club. At night in Crumlin while he was watching over the cells, he would write little songs for T. R. Dallas and Hugo Duncan and, above all, for Brendan Shine, who had a big hit with one of them, *The Rose Of Castlerea*. He started doing his Mid-West Radio show as John Edwards, but someone made a complaint to the Garda authorities that it was improper for a member of the force to be working for an illegal station. There was an investigation, a file was sent down from Dublin, but then someone in charge said that they liked listening to his show and no action was taken.

John introduces the contestants one by one and has a few words with each before their set. Jackie, a local teacher, sings and plays the Celtic harp and wants to say hello over the radio to Father Stephen and all the First Years in the convent. Pauline from Ballagh sings Chris de Burgh and says that a Nancy

Griffith song 'reminds me of Ireland and the troubles we have here – if we work together maybe we can solve them'. Dave from Kilbeggan has a matching hankie and tie and sings songs made famous by Joe Dolan, 'a man who I've admired and loved for years'. John reads out a request for a girl 'who celebrates her birthday tomorrow and is off to America in the morning'.

And there is this black guy on stage, a black Irishman called Luke Davis who comes from Westport and wears a really cool suit with rolled-up sleeves and no tie. His voice is extraordinary, a cross between Desmond Dekker and Rod Stewart. He purrs and shouts and growls. He sings his own composition with just an acoustic guitar accompaniment. He poses and prowls. He's as Irish as anyone, but here in the Midas there is something foreign and exotic about him. Something that must be kept at a distance. When the judges, local teachers and journalists and businessmen, come to vote for the prizewinners, no one places him first, second or third. He's all very well, very original, but he's not really an all-round entertainer, more a speciality act. Somewhere, hovering around the conversation, is Halal.

'Now remember, girls, when I come back, I'm not Paul Claffey, I'm the man of your dreams . . .' Paul Claffey disappears offstage while the ads are playing on Mid-West Radio, then bounds back on to tumultuous applause. The music this time is the theme from *Rocky*. Around his neck Paul has a bow tie that lights up, little yellow and red lights that flash on and off. Behind him, to the right of the stage, the spotlight picks out a towering white altar of consumer goods, the icons of the affluent society stretching fifteen feet into the air.

Copper electric kettles, microwave ovens, electric underblankets, barbecues, hoovers and boilers are stacked on top of glistening white fridges and glittering white washing machines, all topped by a huge banner proclaiming the name of the sponsor: 'M. Gunning. TV Video/Elect. Equip.' On the left of the stage a day-glo sign, yellow letters on red background, says

'Come On Down...' On the right a matching sign says 'The Price Is Right!' Behind the stage a vast video screen, which will be used to show the items whose prices the contestants are to guess, proclaims again the name of the sponsor. Just offstage, one of the technicians holds up a sign that simply says 'Applause'.

Paul makes his way into the crowd to pick out four contestants. 'Don't be hiding, don't be embarrassed. We have spectacular prizes.' He calls out numbers which correspond to those on big yellow stickers that everyone has been given on the way in: 537, 29, 751, 824. As the contestants gather he shakes a tube over each one and they are showered with coloured party streamers. Ushering them on to the stage, he keeps up a steady stream of patter. 'Anything up here you fancy besides myself? My mother said I was good-looking. Am I?' And the crowds roar back 'No'. 'If you folks at home could see me, I look fabliss: white suit, yellow tie, purple shoes. Don't I look fabliss?'

Mary from Dunmore, Margaret from Carrick, Catherine from Castlerea and Michael, also from Castlerea, line up facing the audience. It is Michael's last night in Ireland before he emigrates to New York. For Catherine, too, it is a special night – this particular weekend is a bank holiday in England, so her husband is home for a few fleeting days with herself and her children. In this setting, the domestic appliances that flash upon the video screen watched by a thousand pairs of eyes have a peculiar poignancy, acting as images of domestic bliss and harmony that for many in this crowd, full of emigrants who are weekend trippers in their own town, are as evanescent and taunting as a game show prize. Paul Claffey knows that the audience he is facing is one that needs dreams. 'I keep the admission charges for the show down to £2.50 because I have to. If they had the money, there's no better man to get it out of them than me, but they haven't.'

Mary is the first to go out when she guesses that a Zanussi washer-drier would cost £1,365. 'It's about time', says Paul, 'I

137

put a bit of culture into this ignorant game.' A massive sow and ten piglets flash up on to the screen, rooting around in a pen. For a minute or two a thousand people in their Sunday best sit in the dark and watch eleven pigs nosing around while the contestants guess how much they would cost. Michael's guess of £550 is the furthest off the mark, so he goes out of the game. 'Sure, what would you know about pigs and you from the town of Castlerea? Tell all on Seventh Avenue we said "Hi" from the Midas.'

Even though Margaret and Catherine knew a lot about the price of pigs, Paul greets the arrival on screen of an outfit from Chic Boutique, Castlerea, with the remark that 'Now, girls, this is genuinely something that you might know something about.' Again, the image is of family togetherness, the outfit described as being 'ideal for a wedding or a special occasion'. After this round, only Catherine is left, which means that she gets to pick a number for a prize. Paul urges her to consult her husband, he shouts up for a number and they win (drum roll, fanfare, huge cheer) a microwave oven. The band plays *Congratulations*. 'You must be thrilled,' says Paul. 'No need to cook his dinner now, just pop it in and press the button.' He doesn't know that these days Catherine's husband has his dinner in England. Outside, in the early hours of Monday morning, something is already stirring at the factory and the sweet, over-rich smell of flesh and offal and hide is already hanging in the darkness.

By eleven in Halal, some of the men who were at the Midas until the small hours are already into double figures, slitting sheep's bellies, peeling back the skin so that the head hangs curiously upside down detached from the body that is already on the way to becoming a commodity, pulling out the guts with their hands and putting intact stomachs into a great vat on wheels with all the other stomachs. The pace is hectic, though methodical and matter-of-fact, but the sights are nonetheless strange: men stamping flesh with little blue harps like official documents, men loading vast rows of carcasses on hooks into cavernous trucks, men, on this May day, working in woollen hats, thick blue jackets with big padded gloves, their faces appearing eerily out of the ice-room fog, their feet planted on thin layers of iced-over concrete. And all, after a night of country and western and American game shows, working away in the name of Allah.

Down the road, in a tiny room at the back of the Midas, Paul Claffey is already back at work, hosting his regular morning show on Mid-West Radio. On his sound desk is a trophy made by a local business to be given away to the winner of yesterday's Cow Plop Contest in Bekan, a few miles away on the road to Claremorris. The trophy has a cow on the top and a large round cake that looks like cow-dung on the bottom. 'Still trying to find out exactly what happened at the cow-ploppin' yesterday. If you won the contest ring us and collect this fabulous award ... In the meantime, here's one from Barry Manilow.' The Cow Plop Contest was one of the main attractions at the Bekan Family Day whose delights also included Ladies and Gents Tug-O'-War, Guess the Weight of a Sheep, Hammer the Nail, Throw the Wellington and Best Dressed Dog. For the Cow Plop, a field is marked out in numbered squares, each entrant is given a number and the one which corresponds to the square in which the cow first defecates wins £250.

As the morning progresses, there is more urgent business. 'There's a dog missing from the Toureen/Kilkelly area, a black smooth-hair collie with a white front leg. Answers to Simon, missing since Friday.' There is the No Belly Award for Paul's Plumps, women trying to lose weight. 'Please don't be angry with me,' writes one who has succumbed to temptation, 'as I just couldn't bear it! I feel so bad as it is, after letting you down.' There are items for sale: 'a large dress with beaded pearls, size 14', 'a fast tanning sunbed, little used'. There are quizzes – 'What is in every house, has a key to open it, and is made in Tubbercurry?' There is a woman who has 77 Calvita tokens for a trip on the B&I and wants to sell them. There are greetings for girls home from England for the weekend. And there are songs. One of the most requested is Red Sovine's *Teddy Bear*, about a trucker 'on the outskirts of a little Southern town' who gets the voice of a little boy on his CB. 'I get lonely and it helps to talk/'Cos that's about all I can do/I'm a cripple, you see, and I can't walk ... Dad used to take me for rides when he was home/But I guess that's over now he's gone.'

Another of the most popular records is *The JCB Song* sung by Seamus Moore. It's popular because, in the way that such songs used to mention every town in Tipperary or Mayo, it gets a long list of the pubs in Camden Town into its chorus: The Galtee, Nelly's, The Bell, The Crown ... In the same room where it is being broadcast, the one with the pictures of the Pope, Louise Morrissey and T. R. Dallas on the walls, Brother Gregory stood the previous night. He teaches in the Marist Brothers in Castlerea and is director of the Castlerea Musical Society. He was talking enthusiastically about his last production, *Guys and Dolls*, less so about the increasing difficulty of finding enough young people to make up the cast. The door opened and his face brightened. In walked a young man of around twenty, his star dancer, one of the great hopes for his next production. 'I'm delighted to see you,' he said. 'I've just the part for you ...' The young man looked at him as if he were touched. 'What? Me? Don't you know? I've been in London for the last six months. I'm only here for the weekend. I'm not here at all.'

1988

The Irish for Ho Ho Ho

For a few years now, I have been Santa Claus in the Christmas fete at my sons' school. I approach the job with mixed feelings.

On the one hand, it is chastening to realise that only in a red suit with two pillows shoved up inside the jacket and with most of my face hidden by an itchy white beard can I manage to look benevolent and cheerful instead of cynical and lugubrious. On the other, the experience is strangely and wonderfully touching. It makes you realise that there is still a capacity for wonder in the world.

Santa's grotto is usually in the corner of a familiar classroom, marked off with a makeshift arrangement of black plastic bags, crepe paper and tinsel. Virtual reality it isn't. Entering this somewhat tacky domain to find a stooped and suspiciously thin figure with absurd strands of some synthetic fibre straddling his harassed-looking face and pathetic wisps of greying hair peeping out from under his hood, any self-respecting four-year-old, steeped in Bart Simpson's streetwise cynicism, ought to raise the alarm.

The astonishing thing is that very few of them do. There is always the odd nine-year-old wiseguy, but the pressure of a heavy Santa-type toecap on a Nike-trainered toe usually ensures silence. Mostly, from the younger kids, there is the purest and most naked awe. And from the older ones there is something more remarkable still – a conscious decision to be fooled. They can see the awkward illusion for what it is, but they actually choose to go along with it, to play out a ritual that, for all its dodgy exterior, still has for them an inner meaning.

The fact is that in an age when few rituals, even very serious ones, can retain their force, Santa Claus still works. And it is not just the story – the cosy narrative of snow-bound toy factories, elves, reindeer, chimneys and stockings – that works, but also the visual code. Even in the most unpromising of circumstances, with an aging journalist in a second-hand suit sitting in a corner of a draughty classroom, the suit, the beard, the hood, the boots, the belt, the bulging belly, have an irresistible allure.

And the interesting thing is that this visual code is itself neither very old nor very hallowed. It was invented in its finished form – the red suit with white trimmings, the white beard, the twinkly old eyes – in the 1930s by an artist commissioned to create an image of Santa Claus for a Coca Cola advertisement. That image itself drew on the promiscuous range of cultures thrown into the American melting pot: Saint Nicholas from Asia Minor via Holland, Scandinavian pagan legends of Yule Buck, Father Christmas from England.

For cultural purists, Santa was a nightmare, an example of modern inauthenticity at its very worst. Irish cultural nationalists were no exception, and though it is now forgotten, one of their projects was to replace Santa with an authentic Gaelic figure. For Christmas 1917, the Irish Ireland movement produced T. H. Nally's *Finn Varra Maa – The Irish Santa Claus* at the Theatre Royal. It was, as its title suggested, a conscious attempt to repel the invasion of the alien Santa.

Early in the play, the old granny – there was always an old granny – sings a song which includes the lines

> *In England they have one they call 'Father*
> *Christmas'*
> *A grey-bearded Russian they dub 'Santa Claus',*
> *But here in the fair land of Erin we dismiss*
> *Their Muscovite fairies with white-whiskered jaws.*
> *They've stolen our Poetry, Music, and Stories,*
> *Our orators, statesmen, our letters and art*
> *But they shall not rob us of our ancient glories*
> *They're guarded too well in each true Irish heart.*

142

The production was bedecked with the standard images of Ireland – thatched cottages, spinning wheels, bog-deal dressers, and a wolfhound of whom the *Evening Herald* noted: 'The wolfhound squatting on his haunches and occasionally biting himself was nobly Irish . . .'

Instead of Santa, true Irish children were to expect a visit from Finn Varra Maa. Finn would come down the chimney at midnight and leave toys made by fairies. But he would live the rest of the year not in the alien North Pole but in Connemara. He would wear not a red suit and a fluffy beard but a fairy cloak and hat. And since there was no mention of reindeer, he would travel, presumably, by ass and cart.

All of this was not entirely laughable. The idea that people should have their own culture, their own images of benevolence and goodwill, was by no means unreasonable. But to judge from contemporary reviews, it may have been somewhat boring. The *Evening Herald* applauded the idea and tried very hard to make it all sound exciting, but wondered in an aside 'whether it is not a little too simple for our average Irish theatre-goer, brought up on the "guffawed" goods imported from across the channel'. Even 80 years ago, the idea of cultural purity was a bit too simple for most Irish people.

Poor Finn, of course, never caught on, probably because he missed the point – that spirits are meant to be, not familiar and authentically rooted in native soil, but strange and exotic. But probably also because it is exactly the mongrel nature of Santa Claus, his lack of a proper pedigree, that makes him so resonant. He is everything that an enduring icon should not be – synthetic, manufactured, makey-up. But he is a great celebration of accidental cultural collisions, of glorious impurity. He lives in the North Pole because he comes from nowhere, and coming from nowhere can belong everywhere.

The fact is that when it comes to symbols, most of us would prefer Santa's flying reindeer any day to a nobly Irish wolfhound sitting on his haunches and occasionally biting himself.

Authentic cultures do tend to end up gnawing on their own tails, turning inwards with puritan disdain on themselves. Images that are obviously invented, on the other hand, are infinitely open. Santa works because people, whatever their cultures, can still make an image their own, can still invest it with personal meanings and emotions, and still have a capacity for hope and wonder that transcends the evidence of their eyes.

Like the children who reckon that Santa doesn't exist, but choose to believe in him anyway, cultures can learn to enjoy operating on more than one level at the same time. They can believe in the authenticity of things even if they are impure. Given the consequences of the pursuit of cultural purity in both parts of Ireland, they know that those who can't manage such an act of faith will wake up to a sack of ashes.

1996

Gay Byrne

Voices from the Silence

The man sipped, replaced his pint on the bar counter and glanced through the haze of cigarette smoke at the television screen. The shot on the screen moved from a close-up of Gay Byrne's face to a wide view of the audience. The man froze for a moment, then grabbed his coat and pushed furiously through the doors on to the street, leaving his half-finished pint on the counter. Back in the pub, Gay Byrne's voice continued to mingle with the Saturday night chinwag, with the passion and the trivia, with the vital questions of the day and the chit-chat that would not outlive the night.

A short while later in Montrose, the *Late Late Show* audience was streaming out into the pouring rain. Many were sheltering under the colonnade in front of the studio when they heard the screams. The security staff heard them too and rushed to Montrose House, just across the grounds from the studio entrance. There, on the steps of the old house, they found the man from the pub brandishing a knife, threatening another man while a woman screamed. The man with the knife had seen something he did not expect to see on the *Late Late Show*: his wife in the audience with another man.

He had suffered a more extreme version of the things that had outraged, delighted, entertained and disturbed Irish people since Gay Byrne began to present the *Late Late Show* in 1962: the revelation of intimacies in the glare of the studio lights, the disclosure in public of things that had never been disclosed in private. For once, that wet winter's night, the show outside the

145

studio was brasher, more dramatic and more spectacular than the one inside.

Gay Byrne's extraordinarily central place in the Irish life of the past three decades is due not to his own obvious skills – the flow of language, the plausibility, the urbanity – but to their opposite: to the culture of silence which surrounds them. 'I have never', the letters to him say, 'told this to anyone in my life . . .' 'I feel very depressed at times and wish I could reveal my secret to somebody . . .'

'That was ten years ago and since then my mother and I have never mentioned it . . . Please don't use my name or address as I couldn't stand it if the neighbours knew . . .'

It is the silences that have made Gay Byrne what he is in Ireland: the silences at the breakfast table, the silences around the fireside, the silences on the pillow. Without them he would be what he so patently is – a superbly professional broadcaster, confident, adaptable, quick thinking and fast talking – and no more. With them, he is something else altogether: the voice in which the unspoken can be articulated, the man who gives permission for certain subjects to be discussed. His is the voice, calm, seductive and passionless, in which things that would otherwise be unbearable can be listened to, things like this letter which he read on the radio in February 1984: 'When I learned that the thing that happened between men and women, as it was locally known, had happened to me, I slowly realised that I might also be going to have a baby . . . In terror and panic, I tried to find out from newspapers any snippets of information. I learned that babies like the one I might have were usually placed in brown paper bags and left in a toilet and I resolved to do this . . . For that reason, I started to carry around the one penny I would need to get into the toilet to have the baby . . . I kept the brown paper bag in my schoolbag and kept the bag under my bed at night . . . Since I spent most of my time in the chapel praying, the nuns told me I had a vocation.'

Surrounded by that silence, we wanted, in the 1960s, to hear ourselves speak in a charming, sophisticated and worldly-wise voice. And here was a man who had made it in England with Granada TV and the BBC but still wanted to come home, a man who could talk on equal terms with suave foreigners and still be one of our own, who could mention sex and nighties and contraceptives and still be a good Catholic. It is significant that the thing most frequently said about Gay Byrne's broadcasting style, by himself and by others, is that he asks the questions that the audience at home would want to ask but wouldn't dare. His achievement is founded on Irish people's inarticulacy, embarrassment and silence, on speaking for us because we were – and to a degree still are – afraid to speak for ourselves.

If we're too embarrassed to have a national debate about contraceptives, the *Late Late Show* will do it for us. If we're too shy to harass the fellow who sold us a dud washing machine, the Gay Byrne Show will harass him for us. If we're too ashamed to tell our friends that our husbands haven't spoken to us for twenty years, Gay Byrne will tell the nation for us. And however much pain may go into such letters, just hearing them read in that smooth, warm, sophisticated voice already transforms the pain into something cool and clean and modern, into another masterly performance. We have been, literally, making a show of ourselves, with Gay Byrne as the cast of thousands.

His presence is now so all-pervasive that it is easy to forget that the first star of the *Late Late Show* was not Gay Byrne but television itself. Gay Byrne has explained that the initial idea for the show was that its ambience should be that of an evening around an Irish country fireside with the young master entertaining his guests. The image was one out of de Valera's Ireland, out of the lexicon of the man who had opened RTE itself a few months before the *Late Late Show* went on the air as a temporary stop-gap.

What de Valera had imagined television to be like was made clear in that opening address. He saw it as presenting 'the good, the true, the beautiful': 'the masterpieces of architecture, engineering, sculpture, painting … the great musical compositions of the great composers'. 'I find it hard to believe', he said, 'that a person who views the grandeurs of the heavens, or the wonders of this marvellous world in which the good God has placed us, will not find more pleasure in that than in viewing, for example, some squalid domestic brawl or a street quarrel.' But Gay Byrne didn't present the *Late Late Show* as cosy fireside chat. On the contrary, and long before it became the fashion in television elsewhere, it went out of the way to make television itself a star, showing the wires, the lights, the monitors, the cameras, the technicians, and, of course, the hero of the hour, the audience.

It celebrated television as the very image of modernity, of technology, of all the things we were trying desperately to become. And as it went on, it filled itself with domestic brawls and street quarrels, with battered wives and Bernadette Devlin fresh from the barricades, presenting the good, the true and the beautiful only insofar as they added to the mix, kept the audience amused and the TAM ratings up. If the Gay Byrne who was doing this had not existed, he would most emphatically not have been invented, for the *Late Late Show* was doing precisely what those in authority thought that television should not do. What those in authority did not understand, and what Gay Byrne lived for, was the logic of a good show, the fact that fireside chats and the masterpieces of architecture put the plain people of Ireland to sleep, while brawls and revelations kept them up and watching.

The authorities – the bishops, politicians, county councillors, GAA officials, Vocational Educational Committees – realised very quickly what was afoot, but they had great difficulty in doing anything about it. It is significant that, of all the avalanche of protests that began in 1966 when a hapless woman called Eileen Fox revealed on the show that she had worn nothing on the night of her honeymoon and continued when Brian Trevaskis called the Bishop of Galway a moron, very little was directed at Gay Byrne personally. The objects of attack were television in general, the *Late Late Show*, RTE.

The show could be described by Loughrea Town Commissioners as 'a dirty programme that should be abolished altogether', or criticised by Meath VEC for its 'mediocrity, antinational tone and recently low moral tone', but the objectors knew better than to accuse Gay Byrne himself of being dirty or morally low and were thus left flailing at abstractions. Gay Byrne's personality was crucial in that he became an Irish Everyman, spanning the past and the present, the traditional and the modern. Neat, sober and kind to old ladies, he was the son every Irish mammy would like to have had. Suave, brash and upwardly mobile, he was the man every mother's son dragging himself up by his bootstraps would like to be.

Only two aspects of Gay Byrne's personality (as opposed to his professional skills) are important to his broadcasting achievement, but both are essential to the survival of his show. The first is that his own life represents in microcosm much of what has happened to Ireland in the past thirty years. Brought up in a sheltered, frugal and conservative family environment. Inculcated by the Christian Brothers with the values of piety, hard work and patriotism. Emigrating to England along with everyone else in the 1950s. Coming back along with everyone else in the 1960s. Getting richer as the country gets richer. Suffering financial calamity in the 1980s and contemplating emigration again.

His personal odyssey, then, has followed the same course as the national epic, the same serpentine currents of hope and despair, of excitement and boredom. Because he had been shaped by those conflicting currents, he can be compared by one person to the leader of godless communism, by another to a Christian Brother. Senator J. B. Quigley saw him as Stalin: 'Like Khrushchev, I am all against the cult of the personality.' June Levine saw him as often 'like a Christian Brother of the nasty type Irishmen have described to me: merciless, unreasonable, relentless in his attack on anyone who fell short'. What he is most like, though, is contemporary Ireland – fluid, contradictory, elusive, a country in which the terms either/or are replaced by the terms both/and. Gay Byrne, like his country, is both traditional and modern, both conservative and liberal, both Catholic and materialist. The relative emptiness of his public persona is his greatest strength, keeping him from freezing in any set of unified attitudes, keeping him close to the irregular pulse of Irish life.

The other aspect of his personality that is important is related to this emptiness: the fact that he is, at heart, an actor. From a very early age, he wanted to act, and it was in the drama academies and the Dublin Shakespeare Society that he created himself as a performer. It is very doubtful if he would have had the emotional commitment, the imaginative sympathy, to be a really good actor, but it is the playing of roles which still keeps him going. On the one hand, there are the funny voices, the prancing around the studio with a contraceptive cap on his head, the willingness to have darts thrown at him or to have a melon on his chest chopped in half with a samurai sword. This aspect of his showing off has preserved his shows as Light Entertainment, making the more serious and unpalatable parts of them just a part of the package in which the junkie with AIDS will be followed by a song and dance – after the commercial break.

The other side of the acting is the detachment, the coldness. He can ask the hurtful, nasty, embarrassing questions because it is in the script, because it is the role he is playing, because the interviewee is playing a part, too, and is not to be thought of as a bundle of real fears and emotions. R. D. Laing is drunk and crumbling in front of the cameras: confront him with his drunkenness and shuffle him off. E. P. Thompson, at the time the most influential intellectual in Europe as leader of European Nuclear Disarmament, is getting a bit complicated: cut him off after a few minutes, turn to the model from *Celebrity Squares* who was the previous guest and get her to talk about nuclear disarmament instead. Ask Des O'Malley about his meeting with Charles Haughey during the Arms Trial, ask Father Bernard Lynch if he's gay. Don't flinch, don't hedge, don't even change the tone of voice. How, the victims ask, can he be so nice one moment and so nasty the next? The answer is that neither the niceness nor the nastiness is anything personal, just a change of roles.

It is the slippery quality, this refusal to be fish of flesh, one thing or the other, that his enemies have always recognised as Gay Byrne's most dangerous quality. His one consistent credo, the one thing in his public persona which could be described as a principle rather than an attitude, is that it is in the nature of television to throw everything in together, to refuse to recognise the distinctions between entertainment and seriousness, and that the medium, rather than any set of rules, has to be respected. 'When the new toy called television came to Ireland,' he recalled in an interview in the gay magazine *OUT* a few years ago, 'we had to recruit a whole new crop of people, young people, to come in and run it because the old school of radio did not know how to run this new thing, this new machine. Those new people had none of the ethics or ethos which would have been picked up in Radio Eireann and they saw no reason why we should not examine all the topics and the controversial issues and the things which affected people in real life, rather than the imaginary things that affected imaginary people.'

This tendency to see television as something which makes its own rules as it goes along has been resisted from the start. The most consistent tack of those who find Gay Byrne uncomfortable is to demand, not that he be removed, but that he be defined: serious or entertaining? 'Telefís', wrote the TV critic of the *Irish Catholic* in 1966, 'has the responsibility to define which programmes are suitable for responsible expressions of views of important controversial content and which programmes by

151

their nature are unsuitable for this ... If the *Late Late Show* is to become a place for expression of views in which selected guests can say what they like, then it must be acknowledged and prepared as a serious discussion programme ... There would have to be a chairman who preserves a balance rather than throw in innocuous comments or asides which amount to an uneasy handwashing ... If, on the other hand, it is not intended to be such, but to be merely a form of entertainment, then it must be controlled so that nobody uses it, no matter how sincerely, for soap box oratory.'

Sixteen years later, almost exactly the same argument was being made by Fred O'Donovan, then Chairman of the RTE Authority, when he banned a *Late Late Show* discussion on the abortion referendum. 'Because of the emotional situation with cameras, people say things they wouldn't normally say. This is too important a subject to be treated trivially.' The same things had happened before – in 1968, when the show was prevented from discussing a biography of Eamon de Valera on the grounds that it would be 'inappropriate in the context of the *Late Late Show*' and again was prevented from broadcasting a programme on the defeat of the government in a referendum on proportional representation. The implicit message was always the same: if serious things were to be discussed, they should be discussed on serious, predictable programmes where the ground rules had been worked out in advance. Gay Byrne's openness and unpredictability were dangerous because people might 'say things they wouldn't normally say'.

Government ministers, particularly Fianna Fáil ministers, have always been reluctant to be interviewed by Gay Byrne, not so much because they are afraid he will make them say things they'd rather not have said, but because his whole style refuses to recognise them as fundamentally different from the knife-thrower or the film star. To submit to Gay Byrne is to submit to being treated as Entertainment, to being stripped of office, record, power, everything except your ability to hold the audience's attention for five minutes or 50 minutes. Pan Collins, the former *Late Late Show* researcher, once wrote that her job was 'to produce a list of possible guests under six different headings: an intellectual, a glamour personality, a VIP, a cynic, a comic and a cookie character'.

But in Gay Byrne's hands, the borderlines between those categories fall away. The intellectual of one shot can be made the cookie character of the next. The cynic who performs well can become a glamour personality in the space of a few minutes. The VIP who tries to be pompous ends up as the unintentional comic. Where a current affairs programme like *Today Tonight* treats people according to the category it finds them in – expert, economist, political leader, victim – the *Late Late Show* makes and unmakes the categories as it goes along, treating people by their performance, not their past record. Gay Byrne, the man who made his way up in Irish society solely through his ability to entertain, has always presented entertainment as uncomfortably egalitarian. Anyone can speak so long as they speak entertainingly enough. Anything can be said so long as it's gripping enough.

The late Archbishop Kevin McNamara probably had the *Late Late Show* and the *Gay Byrne Show* in mind when he bemoaned the loss of traditional authority in Irish society in 1985: '[There are] certain topics which have exercised the greatest minds for centuries, and on which a fund of traditional wisdom has been built up slowly and with difficulty over the years. These today are regarded as suitable topics for chat shows, on radio and TV, in which speakers of little or no qualifications parade with confidence the most varying and contradictory opinions . . .' He was, of course, right to be concerned, for, in Gay Byrne's pluralist republic of entertainment, the bishop owes his authority not to tradition but to his ability to sing an oul' song and the politician's power can be diminished by his inability to tell a good yarn.

Though not, of course, a yarn like this one:

Two days before Good Friday, in that year, it was potato-setting day. This was the 1940s and all the potatoes were still sown by hand, so everyone had to help, including Mary, who was heavily pregnant. Mary was the servant girl who worked thirteen hours a day, cleaning, cooking, milking, feeding, who was twenty-eight years old and a beautiful singer, who had made love to a man in a nearby village with nine children of his own. Just before dinner time, Mary rushed into the house to help with the serving. She had no dinner herself, complained of a blinding headache, and asked for an hour or two off to go to bed.

After an hour or so, Mary's employer called to her bedroom door. The door was locked, but Mary called through it that she was much better and would be up shortly. After another hour, the house was filled with the screams of a new baby. The woman of the house got her husband, who went a few miles away and fetched Mary's elderly father. Mary still had the door locked and after they forced it down, she denied everything. They searched the room and found a little baby boy choked by a stocking, and Mary packed with her clothes in her suitcase. Mary's father walked her home and carried the case, in which, later that night, the baby was buried. Mary went back to work two days later and that was the end of the matter. She got no help or care; 'it didn't', the letter said, 'exist then'.

We wouldn't know Mary's story without Gay Byrne, who included it on February 23rd, 1984, in the most devastating piece of broadcasting yet heard in Ireland: 50 almost uninterrupted minutes of letters unleashed by the death in childbirth of Anne Lovett in Granard. By then, Gay Byrne's centre of gravity had shifted from television to radio, from the dramatic to the confessional, just as the centre of national debate had moved from the public to the private. By then, a woman who did wear a nightie on her honeymoon would be the cookie character and soon the Leader of the Opposition rather than a Trinity student would be calling bishops names. The exposed nerves were now in more intimate and more painful places.

That programme let it all fly in a controlled but relentless onslaught of terrible intimacies. A sort of secret history of modern Ireland emerged that day with stories from every decade since the 1940s, stories that had been told to no one, stories that had been bottled up and swallowed down. There was only one person in Ireland to whom those stories could be told: someone who had been around long enough to become part of the national conscience, someone who had been pushing back, bit by imperceptible bit, the limits of what could be said in public, someone who was professionally unshockable, someone who was yet so unknown that his judgement or retribution need not be feared – Gay Byrne. It was to our shame that there was no one else to speak to, to our shame that we needed Gay Byrne so much. It was to his credit that he had survived long enough to be there when he was needed.

In the last of those letters, the writer concluded: 'We did not wish to be nosy, but merely to share in their sorrow, as indeed we should.' Much of the time over the past three decades, Gay Byrne has fed our nosiness and fed off it. But at his best he has helped us to share in the sorrow, as indeed we should. Perhaps, out of that sharing, there will come a day when we can hear our intimacies in a voice that doesn't come from the radio, can speak to each other in tones other than Gay Byrne's. On that day, if it comes, Gay Byrne will become what he hasn't been for twenty-seven years: an ordinary broadcaster.

1989

Permission to Speak

There seems to be a general consensus that there is too much talk on RTE and that Gay Byrne has had his day. Both of these perceptions may be accurate enough in themselves, but something tells me that there is, behind them, a deeper disgruntlement. Both Gay Byrne and RTE have played critical roles in the opening up of discussion in Ireland. They have, over four decades, redefined what it is permissible to talk about. And I get the feeling that, for many people, that process has gone far enough. A lot of what we have had to talk about has been very unpleasant indeed, and we are tired of listening to it. We wonder if it would not be better if, after all, the worms were to crawl quietly back under the stones. A court report I read last month made me think again about this.

In September 1993, I went on the *Late Late Show*. I had been writing about the Stay Safe programme in schools and the campaign against it by right-wing Catholic groups. The programme is aimed at giving children a language in which they can discuss bullying and abuse, and an idea of how to report it. It is now being used successfully in virtually every primary school in the Republic, but at the time there was a very strong and well-organised campaign to oppose it. Some of the opponents subsequently came to greater public prominence in the No Divorce campaign. Others are Catholic priests, concerned, as one of them put it, that 'the claim that a child owns its own body is at odds with Christian tradition'.

When I was asked to debate the issue on the *Late Late*, I wasn't sure how to respond. I know enough about television to know how crude it can be, how inadequately it deals with complex and sensitive questions, how it can not merely obscure the truth but actively distort it. I was worried about whether such a debate might merely serve to give a platform for the views of obscurantist cranks. I had also, to be honest, grown weary of a subject on which I had said a lot to little effect and thought I had nothing else to say.

I decided, however, to do the show, largely because some of the propaganda used against the Stay Safe programme had been so vile – claiming, for instance, that it was called the Safe Sex programme, and that it 'prepared children for abuse' – that there was a real danger that some parents might have been genuinely frightened by it. But this consideration only just outweighed the misgivings.

After the show, I was still very unsure about whether I had made the right decision. The debate was a typical television set-piece, more concerned with the drama of absolute oppositions than with establishing truths or imparting information. After it, there was a feeling of utter pointlessness. Here was an issue which, to me at least, could not be more clear cut: whether or not schools should help children to protect themselves from bullying and abuse by talking to adults they could trust.

The discussion seemed, from the inside, merely to have taken that moral clarity and disguised it as yet another round in an endless cultural war between tradition and change in Ireland. That impression was subsequently strengthened by the fact that the campaign against Stay Safe melted away when the divorce referendum appeared on the horizon and the right-wing Catholics moved on to what were, for them, bigger targets.

What I didn't know was that in a housing estate somewhere in County Offaly, an eleven-year-old boy was watching the *Late Late Show* that night with his mother and a neighbour, a man of 75, who usually watched it with them. When the item about the Stay Safe programme came on, the neighbour had become uncomfortable. After a few minutes, he made an excuse and left.

The mother could feel a sense of expectation. Her son then

asked her what sexual abuse was. When she told him, he asked her how she would react if one of her children had been abused. She said she would be supportive. The boy said 'Mammy, I was abused.' He then told his mother that the neighbour who had been watching the *Late Late* with them a few minutes earlier had raped him about twenty times in the previous four years.

The boy had stayed in the neighbour's house to help look after him when he was ill. The man had sometimes plied the boy with vodka or whiskey until he fell asleep and then assaulted him. According to the boy, he also 'told him daft things about men and religion and he told him men could have babies'.

The mother contacted a solicitor shortly afterwards, and she and her son were put in touch with the Midland Health Board. Last September, a complaint was made to the Garda, and last month the neighbour, having pleaded guilty to two sample charges of rape and two of sexual assault, was jailed for five years.

This story is, amongst other things, a tribute to Gay Byrne, whose broadcasting career is now apparently entering its home stretch. It is very hard to think of any other circumstances or any other place in which a 75-year-old man, an eleven-year-old boy and a middle-aged woman would all be sitting down at ten o'clock on a Friday night watching a debate about the prevention of child abuse between an obscure journalist and a barely less obscure academic. And it is very hard to imagine that, after the *Late Late* is gone, any television programme will ever again have the kind of routine place in people's lives that allows for such a direct link between reality and the stylised drama of the small screen.

But the story is also a necessary reminder that there is still, in Ireland, a great deal to be said. Those of us who work in the media become affected by a paradoxical mixture of weary futility and self-centred arrogance in which we both undervalue and over-rate the work we do. We get tired of dealing with the same issues time and again, and often lose the conviction that there is any point in saying them. But we also assume that because we are weary of an issue, its importance has somehow diminished. We forget why it arose in the first place – because it touches the lives of the people we are supposed to serve.

Talking about things does, sometimes, change them, just as refusing to talk about them allows them to happen. The man convicted of rape in Offaly also admitted to Gardai that he had abused his grand-nephew years earlier. He got away with it. That young man went to England where he subsequently suffered a nervous breakdown that halted a promising career. Fifteen years ago, what had been done to him was not a subject for public discussion in the newspapers or on television, and because it wasn't we thought the place was much nicer than it really was. But if it had been, the abuser might not have been free to move on to another victim, and destroy another life. It may be more pleasant to fill the silence with happy music, but there are very good reasons why the tongue set free by radio and television should never be tied again.

1996

No Place Like Home

The last of that immigrant generation have all but slipped away, but the effect of the broad strokes of the comedians and caricaturists has been to tamper with memory. Unthinkingly the descendants accept the stereotypes, and squeeze their ancestors into the narrow and rather condescending mould that others have created for them.
– Ruth Gay, *Unfinished People*

A hundred years ago, in May 1897, an Irish Fair was held at the Grand Central Palace on Lexington Avenue, New York, to raise funds for an Irish Palace Building, intended to contain a library, a shooting range and a riding school. The most popular exhibit was a giant topographical map of Ireland. In a long, rectangular room, surmounted by a huge green shamrock and surrounded by five columned archways, the map was spread across the floor. It was divided into thirty-two parts, each representing the exact contours of a county. But the special attraction of the map was that each of these 'counties' had been filled with 'the veritable Irish soil of the county . . . duly attested as truly genuine'. For ten cents, the visitor to the fair could walk the length and breadth of the island. The Irish immigrant could feel under foot the land itself, the literal ould sod.

As the New York *Irish World* reported, 'many a pathetic scene is witnessed daily'. One day an 80-year-old Fermanagh woman called Kate Murphy paid her ten cents and stepped across the coastline and made for her native county. She knelt down and kissed the soil, 'then, crossing herself, proceeded to say her prayers, unmindful of the crowd around her. While thus kneeling, a photographer took a flashlight picture of her. The flash was a revelation to the simple hearted creature, who seemed to think it a light from heaven, and was awed into a reverential silence. When she finally stepped off the Irish soil, she sighed sadly and clung to the fence, still gazing at "Old Ireland". She kept looking backward as she walked away, as if bidding a long farewell.'

The strange, haunting quality of this event has much to do with its apparent confusion of time and place. It confuses time because, though it happened a century ago, it seems to belong so obviously to the end of the twentieth century: the virtual reality of the re-created Ireland, nature (the real soil 'duly attested as truly genuine') become culture (an exhibit framed, packaged and commodified, available at ten cents a throw), intense personal experiences played out in the artificial glow of camera flashes, signs taken for wonders. A country has become a heritage attraction long before such an idea ought to have gained currency.

And it confuses place because, in a room in a city in another continent, there is still an overpowering sense of Ireland. The very stuff of the land has become not less but more tangible, not more abstract but more real. The soil trodden heedlessly so many millions of times, the earth that was scraped off boots or washed off potatoes, has acquired the awesome magic of authenticity. It matters deeply that the soil was not scooped from a garden in Queens or even shipped in a job lot from Dublin, but carefully gathered in each county.

And those confusions of time and place are central to Irish experience. For the Ireland of the 1990s, there is no straight line of historical development leading from the past to the present. The present generation in Ireland itself is faced with experiences it regards as new – globalisation, multiple identities, imagining society as multiracial and multicultural, living in a media-saturated universe where reality and image are often indistinguishable. And, on the island itself, those experiences are indeed new. But, for previous generations of Irish people, they are not new at all. The Irish men and women who lived in New York and London, in Chicago and Glasgow, have gone through it already. Not just our present but our future is their past. The grand narrative of a society moving from the pre-modern to the modern to the post-modern, breaks down in Ireland.

Consider, for instance, the question of tolerance for other cultures. One of the great paradoxes of Irish history after the foundation of the State is the complete contradiction between the expectation, on the one hand, that Irish people had a right to emigrate to wherever they could, and on the other, the great reluctance to allow immigration into Ireland, even in the extreme circumstances of Jewish refugees fleeing the Holocaust. It is as if there were at one and the same time two Irelands: a pre-modern one contained on the island itself which assumed that the natural state of a culture was one of monolithic purity, and a post-modern one outside the island, able to cope with the global intermingling of race, ethnicity and religion. These two Irelands do not succeed each other in a logical chronological order. The more open precedes the less open.

Thus, for instance, in the 1920s there were no fewer than twenty-two films dealing with relations between the Irish and the Jews in America. The depiction of romances between Irish girls and Jewish boys was almost a stock-in-trade of popular drama. The vogue was inspired by Anne Nichols's 1922 comedy *Abie's Irish Rose*, in which a Jewish boy and an Irish Catholic girl, afraid to tell their parents that they are in love, are married by a Methodist minister. It had 2,327 performances, one of the longest runs in the history of Broadway, and was also turned into a novel (1927), a radio serial (1942) and a movie (1946).

Yet, twenty-three years after *Abie's Irish Rose* opened on Broadway, the idea of allowing any significant number of Jews into Ireland was still anathema. Writing in 1945, S. A. Roche, secretary of the Department of Justice in Dublin, reviewed Irish government policy on the reception of Jewish refugees during the Holocaust: 'The immigration of Jews is generally discouraged. The wealth and influence of the Jewish community in this country appear to have increased considerably in recent years and there is some danger of exciting opposition and controversy if this tendency continues. As Jews do not become assimilated with the native population, like other immigrants, any big increase in their numbers might create a social problem.' Roche subsequently wrote that Jews 'do not assimilate with our people but remain a sort of colony of a world-wide Jewish community. This makes them a potential irritant to the body politic and has led to disastrous results from time to time in other countries.' An image of Irishness that was a commonplace of popular culture in New York was unimaginable in Ireland itself.

The same is true of Irish contact with other races. Irish-American racism has a long and dishonourable history, but there is some reason to believe that later Irish emigrants were more racist than their predecessors. In pre-1870s New York, about a quarter of all Chinese men were married to Irish women. Delinquent Irish and African-American teenagers were brought together in the House of Refuge, a New York reformatory, and often formed lasting relationships. In 1853, the *New York Times* reported that black and Irish waiters had formed a union and gone on strike together.

In the 1840s and 1850s, Irish and black people mixed freely in the Five Points district of New York, bounded by the Bowery to the east and Broadway to the west. Graham Hodges has noted that, in the local bars and dancehalls, 'Irish and black revellers danced, sang and courted to popular melodies composed from European and African rhythms.' In Ned Buntline's 1850 novel *The G'Hals of New York*, an Irishman 'commenced humming, in a low tone, the Negro melody of *Mary Blane*', but 'there was nothing in this to arrest particular attention'.

Charles Dickens, visiting one of the Five Points bars, noted that 'in the negro melodies you catch a strain of what has been metamorphosed from such Scotch or Irish tunes, into somewhat of a chiming, jiggish air'. Accompanied by two policemen on a visit to Peter Williams's tavern in Five Points, Dickens was astonished to see Irish and black men and women dancing, drinking and making love. After Dickens, as Graham Hodges puts it, 'no popular construction of Five Points was complete without a description of a love affair between a black man and an Irish woman'.

In 1850, George Foster, in a guide to the Five Points district, noted the frequency of intermarriage between black American men and Irish women. In one home, for instance, there were two inter-racial couples, John de Poyster, a black labourer, and his wife Brigid, from Ireland, sharing the house with John Francis, a black man from Virginia, and his Irish wife Susan.

And yet, in the early decades of the Irish State, not only was the presence within the nation of black or Chinese people – let alone the idea of sexual relations between Irish women and black men – unimaginable, but even black-influenced music was widely regarded as intolerable. The Gaelic League, launching a renewed anti-jazz campaign in 1934, declared that 'It is this music and verse that the Gaelic League is determined to crush . . . Its influence is denationalising in that its references are to things foreign to Irishmen: that it is the present-day instrument of social degradation is all too plain, even in Ireland. That was the reason for the re-launching of the anti-jazz campaign, the reason it received the blessing of the church and the approval of the State.'

Only recently, in the wake of the collapse of Irish nationalism and Irish Catholicism, and in the context of the Republic's utter openness to global economic and cultural forces, has it become possible for the people who still live on the island to catch up with the experiences of their great-grandparents in the cities of America and, to a lesser extent, Britain. Thus, the best description of Ireland's place in the world at the end of the twentieth century is this description, not of the present, but of the past of the Irish community in New York, given by Ronald H. Bayer and Timothy J. Meagher in their 1996 book *The New York*

Irish: 'Throughout their history in New York, the Irish have been at the border of the ins and outs, interpreting one to the other, mediating, sometimes including, sometimes excluding. They have been both victim and victimiser, "other" and definer of the "other", and, paradoxically, sometimes played both roles simultaneously.'

What is history for the New York Irish is news for the Irish Irish, balanced, in a global society, between the ins and outs, the victims and the victimisers. There is a sense of moving back to the future, of the newest and most astonishing changes – mass media, virtual reality, the fusion of cultures – being a repetition of what is, in the history of emigrants, old hat. There is also a sense that what is most alien, most foreign, is also a kind of homecoming.

The sense, in the Ireland of the 1990s, of things coming home is related to the sense that in our culture 'home' is a word that had no meaning without 'away'. Kate Murphy's passion and prayers, her outpouring of emotion at the touch of her native soil, are possible in New York, not in Fermanagh. The sense of belonging to a place has often been, in modern Irish culture, in direct proportion to one's distance from it: the further away 'home' is, the larger it looms. Home was not the place you were living in, but whatever was least like it. In the Irish countryside, people longed for foreign cities. In foreign cities, they re-imagined an Ireland that had not interested them when they lived there.

Even in traditional Irish culture, there is no easy sense of home as a natural, uncomplicated state of grace, as something that can be taken for granted. The great *sean nós* singer Joe Heaney used to sing a traditional song called *Peigín is Peadar*. He would preface it with a story in which a poor man is six months married when his wife falls pregnant. She tells him that, with a child coming, he will have to go away and earn some money. He gets work with a farmer twenty miles away, and agrees to stay for seven years. At the end of the seven years, he has forgotten his home, and stays another seven. And at the end of that time, he stays another seven.

After twenty-one years, he remembers that he has a home twenty miles away, but has forgotten that when he left his wife was expecting a child. He tells the farmer's wife that he is leaving to go home. She bakes him a cake to take with him, while her husband offers him a choice. Either he can have his wages for the twenty-one years, or he can have what Joe Heaney in his beautiful Connemara English called 'three advices', one for every seven years he spent with them. The man chooses the advices: whatever way the road is, never take the short cut; never sleep a night in a house where there is an old man married to a young woman; never do anything at night you'd be sorry for next morning.

He leaves and, passing a lake, he sees a short cut. He takes it but remembers the first advice and turns back. Later he learns that two robbers have killed a man walking on that short cut. He arrives at a house and, looking in the door, sees a young woman serving supper to an old man. They offer him a bed for the night, but he sleeps in the barn instead. At midnight, a young man calls to the house, and he and the young woman murder the old man. In the morning, the man reaches home and finds his wife in bed with a bearded man. He reaches behind the door for the hatchet they always kept there, and is about to kill them both when he thinks of the third advice. He asks his wife who the man is and is told that it is his son, born three months after he left. They cut the cake for breakfast and inside find his wages for twenty-one years' labour.

Such stories are as old as *The Odyssey*, but they were still being sung by a generation in Ireland that is only now passing. They remind us that home is not, in the experience of ordinary people throughout history, just a familiar place, something to be taken for granted. It is something that has to be worked for and achieved, a goal that can be reached only by circumnavigating, with help and luck, ferocious dangers, unpredictable treacheries both outside yourself and within your own heart. And you need to be armed with advices, with warnings and incantations that form invisible threads for you to follow. The advices that we hope will lead us safe home are what we call a culture.

One of the things that culture reminds us of is that home is much more than a name we give to a dwelling place. It is also a whole set of connections and affections, the web of mutual recognition that we spin around ourselves and that gives us a place in the world. Older languages tend to contain this idea within themselves. In Irish, the terms *sa mbaile* and *sa bhaile*, the equivalents of the English *at home*, are never used in the narrow sense of home as a dwelling. They imply, instead, that wider sense of a place in the world, a feeling of belonging that is buried deep within the word's meaning.

It is particularly true of Irish culture that the imagination itself is inextricable from the idea of home, usually made powerful by the act of leaving it. Looking at 111 letters to and from Irish emigrants to Australia in the second half of the nineteenth century, David Fitzpatrick found that *home* had much more than a literal meaning, often 'evoking an alternative world of recollection and imagination'. In the network of recollection and imagination – remembering the past and inventing the future – that makes a culture, there's no place like home.

A history of emigration gave to Irish culture a particularly sharp realisation of the fact that a home is much more than a house. Fitzpatrick found the word *home* 229 times, on average more than twice in each letter. One woman writing from Queensland used the term thirty times in three letters. And, significantly, the word was used far more often by the exiles than by those who remained in Ireland. Eighty one per cent of the occurrences were in letters from Australia, just 19 per cent in letters from Ireland.

In most cases, *home* was not used to refer to a house, but to

167

a whole social world. Fitzpatrick lists the shades of meaning in these letters: a dwelling place, a household, a neighbourhood, a country, an unspecified place, an address, a place with special characteristics, a place with special emotional associations, a place to return to. 'Home', he found, 'was not only a symbol of shelter and comfort but also a sense of sociability and match-making.' Yet, when the emigrants talked of home in Australia, these larger associations were mostly absent. Adjectives suggesting warmth, comfort or sociability tended not to be used. *Home* came to mean just a household, 'typically used as part of a mundane dichotomy with school, shop or work-place'.

Home became, in Irish culture, not so much the place you were as the place you wanted to be, a place as much imagined as remembered or experienced. 'Home in Ireland', writes Fitzpatrick of the emigrants' letters, 'was both a real and an imagined location. As an economic unit it continued to affect the fortunes of Irish Australians through the transfer of money and gifts as well as the organisation of further movement. As an imagined location, it sometimes took the form of a dwelling, but equally often of a household or neighbourhood buzzing with banter and gossip. As a symbol of comfort, stability and usually affection, it provided an important source of solace for those facing the taxing and insecure life of the emigrant.'

This imagined, symbolic home became, when it was re-imported into Ireland, the touchstone of both politics and religion. And it is also the link between politics and religion, the thread that bound Catholicism and nationalism, Protestantism and unionism, together. Because the idea of a homeland was so steeped in emotion and yearning, it came to be identified with a spiritual home, a land of milk and honey, a paradise both earthly and unearthly. Both Irish traditions – the Gaelic and Catholic one and the British and Protestant one – came to believe that only by making their home territory spiritually pure, dominated by the righteous believers in their own religion, could it be a fitting symbol on earth of the holy homeland in their heads.

And thus a yearning that began as nostalgia has ended, in our own time, as bloody conflict. The roots of the feeling, in exile, in the act of going out into the world and living with people of different races and languages and traditions, were forgotten. A way of writing, of inventing and of imagining, became a way of reading, of imposing, of defending. The job of culture is to make it into a way of writing again, and, appropriately, it is writers who have been searching for ways to do this.

One way of envisaging that task is to think of a culture as a way of measuring and to remember that Ireland has, in recent decades, changed its system of measurement. When I was ten, we started to learn the metric system of measurement at school. Where before we had measured everything by British imperial standards – walking for miles, drinking pints of milk, measuring out the goals for football on the basis that every large step was a yard – now we were to realise that there was a whole other system, neater, more logical, more redolent of the future.

Though we did not understand this at the time, the decision that we should learn about metres and litres was itself highly political, a symbol that we would no longer be ex-colonials, shuffling around imperial prison yards on shackled feet, but Europeans. Ireland was preparing to join the European Economic Community, and we were entranced with the idea that some great transformation was on the way. Once, part of my school homework was to measure in metres and centimetres the ordinary objects around the house: the height of the door, the width of the table, the depth of the kitchen sink. And even writing down their dimensions in this new language of a glossy, standard Europe, the objects themselves seemed transformed, no longer their mundane selves, but promising and full of allure.

For me, part of that allure was a simple but radiant image.

We learned that the metre was a standard measure of distance, and that every metre we measured was a copy of a prototype metre-long metal bar held in the International Bureau of Weights and Measures in Paris. It was a nice thing to know. There was something comforting about feeling that every distance you could ever traverse was a version of the same distance, that every step you could take was in step with all the others around the world. That unseen, inscrutable length of platinum and iridium in a Parisian vault seemed to guarantee that something at least, would always be exact and unchanging. Behind all the transformations of Ireland at the time, the epic shift from a traditional and rural society to a modern and urban one, seemed to lie this new guarantee of continuity and certainty.

That comforting idea – that everything could change and still be continuous – was one way of imagining Ireland. And as I grew up, the metric system suggested another. It came from the fact that even after we had joined the European Economic Community and adopted the new metric system, we all continued to ignore the measurements and use the old ones. Even the Gaelic Athletic Association, the guardian of traditional Irish games like Gaelic football, converted yards to metres and started to call a 50, the free kick that you get when one of the opposing players puts the ball beyond his own end-line, a 45. But everyone went on thinking of it as a 50.

To this day we drink pints of beer, complain that the beach is miles away, ask for so many square yards of carpet. To this day, if I am told something in metric figures, I have to work out what it would be in imperial figures before it has any meaning for me. And that is a second way of imagining Ireland: that if a culture is about the way people measure things, the residue of an old way of measuring hangs around long after it has ceased to have an official existence.

But there is a third way of imagining Ireland suggested by the metric system, and it struck me recently when I discovered the disturbing fact that the way of fixing the length of the metre has, after all, changed. The platinum and iridium bar may still be in Paris, but it is no longer the ultimate definition of distance. These days, distance is measured, quite literally, in time. Since 1983, length is measured by the clock, not the measuring tape. A metre is no longer a version of a precious metal bar in Paris but the distance that light travels in a given infinitesimal fraction of a second. The ultimate point of reference is no longer physically present, no longer fixed and immutable, but itself in frantic motion, a blur of light that covers 300 million metres a second. It is itself a journey.

These three lessons from the metric system each contain a truth about Ireland. It is a country in which change itself provides the only possible continuity. It is a culture whose ways of measuring things are often unofficial, vestigial and unexplicit, even to insiders. And it is, above all, a country whose journeys can no longer be measured by fixed standards, but have to be gauged by their relation to other, imaginative journeys.

It used to be that at all points around the globe, in Boston or in Glasgow, in New York or in London, in Sydney or in Berlin, the emigrant's distance could be measured in relation to a fixed, unchanging standard called Ireland. Somewhere beyond the waters, locked away in a sealed and sacred vault as an ultimate point of reference, there was a solid, stable length of space, an island in the Atlantic standing firm against the waves and wind. Every step the traveller took could be, imaginatively at least, measured in distance to or from that remembered home.

Now, Ireland itself must be measured not with the metres that derive from a fixed, immutable length of metal in Paris, but from the passage of light through time. Ireland has started to imagine itself in the way photographers imagine the world, measuring distance by the motion of light rather than by a fixed, unmoving object. Its imagined metres and centimetres are the marks of human journeys across the landscape. And it is driven by a desire as old as humanity itself but one that is especially strong in the 1990s' world where global connections have made the world no less inscrutable and no more homely. It is the desire for safe passage, the desire for an endless ball of thread with which to mark our way in the labyrinth so that we can always retrace our steps, the desire for true lines through a map of the world.

In November 1995, the Minor Planet Centre in Cambridge, Massachusetts, decided to name Minor Planet 5029, an asteroid recently discovered somewhere between Mars and Jupiter, 'Ireland'. Minor Planet Ireland is far away and virtually invisible to the naked eye and almost nothing is known about its composition. It bears, in other words, a similar relationship to the terrestrial Ireland as the emergent Ireland of imaginative connections does to the physical Ireland in the Atlantic. Spinning in the dark, held in place by the pull of invisible gravity, it is still solid, full of possibilities, and, perhaps, habitable.

In another sense, though, Minor Planet Ireland is not so dreamily comforting. Ireland has long had its human satellites, its exiled communities orbiting the motherland. But it is not so long since people thought that all the planets went round the earth, and had to suffer the psychic shock of finding that it was the other way round. These days, it gets harder to shake off the thought, absurd but insistent, that Minor Planet Ireland, the distant place called after a familiar one, is not the imagined asteroid but the real, green island that used to be at the edge of Europe.

1996